Praise for

Living Well

99 Stories from the Mikveh

Living Well: 99 Stories from the Mikveh *is a moving account and explanation of a central Jewish ritual. To immerse yourself in this book is to be immersed in sacred waters.*

Rabbi David Wolpe, *Sinai Temple*
named the Most Influential Rabbi in America by Newsweek Magazine

Lori Cooper *has gathered for us a remarkable set of stories of lives uplifted and souls touched in the mikveh. What is the mikveh? A place of miracle. And what is this book? A gift to us all.*

Rabbi Ed Feinstein, *Valley Beth Shalom*
author of Tough Questions Jews Ask

Living Well

99 Stories from the Mikveh

Living Well

99 Stories from the Mikveh

∽

Lori T. Cooper

Marking transitions of life from beginning to end

Copyright © 2018 Lori T. Cooper

Cover Artwork by Louise B. Taubman
Book Layout and Design by Rick Lupert
Edited by Claire Brunhild

ISBN: 978-0-9980495-0-2

Published by Hashakah Press
HashakahPress@gmail.com

To Neil, for your extraordinary love and belief in me.

Table of Contents

Acknowledgments

I am grateful for the people who shared their personal stories with me. They have inspired the writing of this book; without them, there would not be a book.

I am grateful for the many people who saw me through this book:

Thank you to my editor, Claire Brunhild, for her gentle and steady guidance, skillful writing, and enthusiasm.

I want to thank Rita Ross, my dear friend and backdoor neighbor, for her insight, creativity, and wisdom.

I would like to thank the following people who, in various ways, helped to make this book a reality: Louise Taubman for her artistry, generosity, and beauty; Craig Taubman, my cheerleader; Dena Blumenthal; Ruth Pincus; and Leah Richman.

To my parents for their love and support.

A special thank you to my husband, Neil; my children, Yonatan and Eliana, Talia and Adam, Tamar and Yoni; and to my grandchildren, who are my delight.

Foreword

Rabbi Neil S. Cooper

The Beginning, the End, and the Resurgence of an Ancient Tradition

Just outside the walls of the Old City of Jerusalem, amidst overturned rocks and ruins, are dozens of *mikva'ot* (plural for mikveh). It did not surprise archeologists to find these. In fact, many *mikva'ot* have been intentionally left unexcavated, for future generations to uncover. During the periods of the First Temple (destroyed in 586 BCE) and the Second Temple (destroyed in 70 CE) dozens of *mikva'ot* were required to accommodate thousands of pilgrims who made their way to Jerusalem each year for a Festival, Shabbat, or other occasion. They would arrive at the Temple with their sacrifices, as specified in the Torah. Before ascending to the Temple Mount, where the altar was located, they first needed to become ritually pure. Most ritual purity was and still is established by immersing in a mikveh.

With the destruction of the Temple in Jerusalem, the pressing need for ubiquitous *mikva'ot* disappeared. Since that time, mikveh usage became the practice of pietists preparing for holidays and other occasions. Mostly, however, use of a mikveh became associated with women, who would use a mikveh monthly to restore their ritual purity following menses. This practice has been scrupulously followed by observant women throughout history. To our knowledge, no Jewish community has ever existed without a mikveh for women to use. Today, the use of a mikveh is essential in order for one to convert to Judaism.

The abrupt end to widespread mikveh use is curious. Although a mikveh has been used by women continually since the destruction of the Second Temple, the vast majority of Jews since that time have neither knowledge nor experience with this ancient practice. In fact, as a rabbinical student, the only mention of mikveh in my studies was in the context of conversion. Yet, in officiating at many conversion ceremonies, it was obvious that even when used for conversion there was great meaning and power in this ritual.

Twenty years ago, in Philadelphia, non-Orthodox rabbis did not have regular access to a mikveh which could be used by rabbis for their conversion candidates. For the sake of the increasing number of conversions we were witnessing, it became clear the Jewish Community of Greater Philadelphia needed a mikveh which would allow all rabbis unfettered use for conversion ceremonies. In addition, rabbis began to wonder if there might be uses for the mikveh beyond the use by women or the use by candidates for conversion. The notion of new uses of a mikveh came not so much from the creative musings of rabbis, but from the origins of a mikveh itself.

The notion of a mikveh, a Jewish ritual bath, literally goes back to the beginning. The Book of Genesis begins when God creates the world in six days. On the third day, God creates mountains and high places in order to separate water and land. As mountains rise, water runs down, gathering below to form lakes, rivers, and seas.

In Hebrew, there is a specific word which describes the collection of the primordial water collected as it runs down naturally and pools. The Torah describes: *yikavu ha-mayim* (the waters were collected). The three-letter Hebrew root of this word, *yikavu*, is the same root of the word "mikveh." A mikveh is a pool filled with water that flowed, as during Creation, without stopping until it was gathered below. It is this unique system of gathering water which defines a mikveh.

Re-Discovering the Mikveh

The variety of uses for which we employ the mikveh today all relate to the notion of transitions. We use a mikveh at points along our life-journeys which call upon us to leave behind cumbersome spiritual baggage, so to speak, and achieve a sense of spiritual cleansing as we begin new chapters in our lives. The connection between a mikveh and the primordial waters of Creation conveys an unmistakable message of renewal and new beginnings.

As the Jewish community spread out geographically and

modernized, use of a mikveh became limited almost exclusively to devout, Orthodox women. Several reasons can be suggested to explain the reason that over time other women have avoided adhering to this deeply ingrained law and tradition. One reason possibly relates to the aesthetics of the experience.

Before water filters and heaters were available, the use of a mikveh was associated with dank, dark, and mildew-scented rooms housing small pools filled with cold, dirty water. This environment was hardly conducive for a spiritually uplifting experience. Such a visit could only have been motivated by a deep commitment to fulfill an obligatory law, no matter how distasteful the experience. Hygienic concerns also dissuaded some from performing this mitzvah.

Perhaps most off-putting, however, was the association of women's ritual impurity with the notion of being unclean. This misunderstanding finds its roots in the King James translation of the Bible, which translates *"tumah,"* ritual impurity, as "unclean." In rejecting the notion of uncleanliness, women rejected the notion of a mikveh as a facility for cleansing. In fact, prior to using a mikveh one bathes. One should be clean before entering a mikveh. Nevertheless, from the erroneous notion of cleanliness, this mitzvah lost relevance and appeal in the light of contemporary understandings of Jewish ritual and the physiology of women.

Furthermore, beyond hygiene and aesthetics, which can explain part of the reason the mikveh fell into disuse, there may be another possibility. The reason the mikveh fell into disuse may be because the ritual is simply too powerful. Only after witnessing the ways our mikveh was used, and the stories which emerged, did I realize the power of mikveh.

To modern sensibilities, total immersion is suspect. We like to know how things work before we "buy in." We want to experience things a little bit at a time. Mikveh immersion does not allow for that. One enters a mikveh as one enters the world: naked, unadorned, and without pretense or protection. There can be no barrier between one's body and the water of a mikveh. In the waters of a mikveh, there is nowhere to hide or pretend.

One enters a mikveh at a moment of transition, during a point when one seeks renewal, during a time to "reboot" our lives, at a moment when one can feel God's presence. For women who use a mikveh monthly, the mikveh marks the transitional moment when the possibility of new life can be contemplated. Brides and grooms use a mikveh for a moment of personal reflection and private transition as partners merge their lives. Those converting use a mikveh as the final ritual step before officially joining the Jewish community.

More generally, a mikveh provides ritualized opportunities for spiritual cleansing. It also provides opportunities for mindful focusing on hopes and goals to which we aspire and for which we pray. One cannot use a mikveh with only one foot in the water. The mikveh asks us to be enveloped, to be totally surrounded, held, and cradled by waters which have held and sustained our ancestors for over 3000 years.

Why This Book?

This small volume contains ninety-nine stories and reflections inspired by the mikveh. With a few exceptions, they recount events which happened at The Mikveh at Temple Beth Hillel–Beth El, in Wynnewood, PA from 2002 to 2018. These selections were chosen from hundreds which convey similar accounts of discovery and spiritual awakening, moments when blessings were celebrated, and times when people drew strength to endure the hardships of life.

The stories are moving and soulful. They will be deeply appreciated, I am certain, by those who read them. Equally important is that together these stories bear witness to the beauty, power, and value of this ancient and quintessentially Jewish tradition.

Preceding immersion we invite those who are planning to immerse to spend some time in private contemplation, using traditional Jewish prayers, Psalms, poetry, or other material to help reflect on the meaning of the moment. Others meditate or simply sit quietly until they are ready. The process of immersion begins as one enters the water, clean, free of any physical barrier between body and water, and mindful of the personal transition before him or her.

In our mikveh, many choose to enter the water before others enter the room, preserving their modesty and privacy. Also, only people of the same gender, invited by the immerser, may enter the mikveh room during that moment. The immersant faces away to immerse three times or more, and recites the appropriate blessings. The mikveh is both about immersion and emergence. We hope that after emerging from the waters of Jewish tradition and blessing, the road ahead with be traveled with confidence, with blessing, and with joy.

Within the American Jewish community we see, at our mikveh and others, a serious and meaningful renewal and resurgence of interest in a mitzvah that had been all but lost in the non-Orthodox Jewish community. I have no doubt that the sensitivity and careful guidance provided by our mikveh director, Lori Cooper, and by those who direct and guide others, will continue to build and deepen commitment to the mitzvah of mikveh. This, in turn, will bring new strength, devotion, and commitment to the Jewish communities we serve.

Rabbi Neil S. Cooper
Founder and Rabbinic Supervisor
The Mikveh at Temple Beth Hillel – Beth El, Wynnewood, PA
Elul 5778/September 2018

Preface

The ritual of marking significant occasions by immersing oneself in water began thousands of years ago, when the mikveh was introduced into Jewish life. Every person coming to the mikveh has his or her own story. This book reflects a collection of sacred moments experienced in the mikveh over the last several years. These are stories I have been given permission to share. Some chose to write their own accounts and others I have shared from a personal perspective. However, all identifying details have been changed to protect the privacy of all involved.

Writing a book where I shared the stories of others, it seemed only fitting to first begin with my own. Twenty five years ago I suffered a period of severe depression. At times, I was able to function. I would take care of my three children and our home, go to work, and outwardly appear to others as a joyful and capable mother, wife, and friend.

But there were hidden, darker times during which the act of getting out of bed seemed a mountain too high to scale. Slowly, after five years, the shadows began receding. As the darkness began to lift, and as therapy, treatment, and medication began taking effect, I could glimpse the colors of light, hope, and faith weaving throughout my life. I began, again, to treasure seeing my children moving forward in their lives, appreciating their successes and their joys as they grew. I could see wonder in the world; I could notice the shades of green in the trees and smell the blooming honeysuckles as I walked along the road to shul. I had reached a point where I could embrace life more fully once again.

In 2002, a community mikveh was built at our synagogue. As founder and rabbinic supervisor of the mikveh operation, my husband, Rabbi Neil Cooper, asked if I would direct the mikveh. My first response was, "absolutely not," although I somehow ended up reluctantly consenting to get the mikveh up and running.

There were endless lists of tedious minutiae to address. Colors: of towels, tiles, flooring and paint. I felt it important that the office and waiting area be warm and welcoming. I became consumed, as well, with elements of the construction, watching the progress, and offering suggestions. I assured the modesty of each user would be scrupulously protected and confidentiality in this holy space would be safeguarded. We all agreed that the mikveh needed to be an attractive space—a setting to which people would enjoy coming, as we explained to the architect—more like a spa than a high school gym. I then began to realize how excited I was as I awaited the mikveh's completion. I had not felt that same sense of anticipation since depression had invaded my spirit years before.

With the irrational fear that I was setting myself up for failure and with great hesitation, I reconsidered the offer to serve as the mikveh's director. I could see this opportunity matched the calling of my soul and cautiously accepted the position during our first week of operation.

My first phone call came from a family who had just adopted a daughter from China. They were determined to welcome her into the family with a conversion before celebrating their first Shabbat together. I created a short ritual in which each parent expressed their hopes and dreams for their daughter. Then they immersed her in the clear, warm waters of the mikveh. After the ceremony, I went home and was so inspired that I recorded the experience, describing it in great detail for myself. Today, I continue to journal, often on a daily basis, narrating powerful experiences and meaningful moments at the mikveh— moments of transition, renewal, rebirth, healing, and celebration in which I have been privileged to participate for the past sixteen years.

Some time around 2006, I decided I wanted to share these mikveh stories with others and started compiling with the intent of creating a book. I proceeded slowly and found myself procrastinating, eventually dropping the project.

In 2017, I attended the Pennsylvania Conference for Women. As one of 12,000 women present, immense excitement flowed through me. I participated in lectures in which extraordinary women spoke on topics of community, connection, inspiration, momentum, and motivation. The brave, independent women modeling their leadership talents during the seminars illustrated how I didn't have to go it alone—partnership and networking would reinforce my efforts.

These incredible women had given me the confidence to finally reach my goal; I was determined to complete my book of mikveh stories! After the conference I felt propelled, energized, and empowered. I knew before the conclusion of that day that I would return to writing my book, a testament to all that has occured at the mikveh and a labor of love for me.

The story of our mikveh has reached scores of rabbis, and thousands of users. I have had the great privilege of sharing transitional moments of so many people. Their openness and generosity enabled me to be present with them. Each ceremony has brought joy, blessing, or satisfaction to our users and, at the same time, has been a source of strength, courage, and hope for me. I am grateful to those individuals and families who have shared these intimate moments. I am grateful to God who has given me strength and brought me to this time of fulfillment and profound satisfaction.

Marriage

Chapter 1

Shoshana

S hoshana was the essence of joy to her family. They had raised her with the simple hope she would marry a Jewish man. Well, Shoshana not only married a Jewish man but she also declared she wanted to keep kosher and learn about Shabbat. Both these Jewish traditions had been part of her childhood but during her college and medical school years, she had drifted away from observing many of the Jewish traditions of her youth.

Once Shoshana had finally finished her residency at a local hospital, she was able to focus on starting a family. Due to the long hours of her medical profession, she hadn't had the time or energy to date. Her closest friend convinced her to meet one of her single friends and that was how she had met Mark. They hit it off immediately and it didn't take long for Shoshana to know he was "the one."

Shoshana's mother, sister, niece, and her maternal grandparents – four generations! – came to the mikveh to celebrate Shoshana's becoming a bride. Both her grandparents were Holocaust survivors, having arrived on the last freighter entering America in 1942.

Each of them had their own recollections of the mikveh. Her grandmother, Hinda, had immersed on the morning of her wedding. Her grandfather, Hesch, would go to the mikveh in Poland with his father every Friday afternoon as part of preparation for Shabbat.

Despite Hinda's and Hesch's experiences of immersion in Jewish tradition, raising children in America had not been the same as raising children in Poland. Even though her grandparents had used the mikveh, Shoshana's mother, Diane, had not used the mikveh before her wedding to Shoshana's father. It had not been a popular custom to observe among her peers at that time. But as she stood beside her daughter, Diane watched with deep curiosity and great pleasure as Shoshana returned to a sacred Jewish ritual.

All of the women accompanied Shoshana into the mikveh room while her grandfather waited patiently for her on the other side of the wood paneled doors.

"The mikveh experience was a very intimate experience for the women I love," Shoshana recounted to me, "I feel fortunate to be surrounded by my loving family."

After Shoshana dressed, her grandfather completed the family ritual by resting his hands upon the bride's head, speaking gently into her ears, and blessing her with the ancient Hebrew words of the traditional Priestly Blessing. ✐

> *May God bless you and guard you.*
> *May God's face shine upon you and be gracious to you.*
> *May God watch over you and bless you with peace.*
>   *Numbers 6:24*

Nancy

*M*y visit to the mikveh was a wet, rainy afternoon I will never forget. There was something indescribable about being in warm waters that mimicked the quiet of the womb and the placid, soothing environment that propelled me forward to earnestly ride the waves of my emotions. While I engaged this ancient and larger-than-life tradition, I didn't know what to expect, and I anticipated the potential to be uncomfortable at being so physically and emotionally exposed. And unexpectedly, I encountered the opposite.

I was uncharacteristically at a loss for words when Lori asked me how I was feeling at the end of my visit. I later shared with her that the word "heavenly" came to mind. I had felt God inside those warm waters and knew God was going to be part of my relationship with my husband-to-be. While in the mikveh, I had glimpsed my new life to come. I envisioned the journey I would soon embark upon days later in a way I hadn't before. ⌒

To live life with another is better than no other.
        Socrates

Shira

S hira grew up in a very observant Jewish household, the daughter of a rabbi. She had rebelled against Judaism and her parents when she graduated college. She didn't like the presumptuous expectations her parents had, whether for her to marry a Jew, to have a certain kind of job, or to practice a particular kind of Judaism. In the end, she fell in love with Dan, a Jewish man who was very committed to his Jewish identity. She felt conflicted about which Jewish rituals to incorporate into her marriage ceremony. Both her parents and Dan wanted to include as many as possible; Shira continuously struggled with her own negative associations around Jewish ritual.

"I thought a lot about going to the mikveh before my wedding," she had shared with me prior to coming. "I wasn't sure what the experience would mean to me."

Shira was surprised at the depth of her reaction to the ritual.

She confided in me afterward, saying, "With each immersion I felt spiritually lifted. By the time I finished my third immersion, my excitement was beyond belief."

As she reluctantly climbed up the seven steps to exit the mikveh, she had said out loud, "I am slowly re-entering the corporeal world."

While Shira packed her things to leave, she curiously asked me about how she could discover the same spiritual feeling from the mikveh again under the *chuppah,* the Jewish marriage canopy.

"Maybe I am re-entering the Jewish world, too," she quietly observed. ✐

Isaac dug anew the wells that had been dug by
his father Abraham.
                      Genesis 26:16

Jean

*J*ean's South African accent always made her sound exotic. We had bonded years before when she joined her daughter, Anna, at the mikveh before Anna's wedding. She had recently invited me to her home for tea and to admire Anna's wedding photos. It was also a perfect time for us to catch up on each other's lives. Her home was full of African artifacts: pottery sculptures of animals from the Serengeti and Jewish ritual items like brass candlesticks from her European grandparents.

"The mikveh was such a unique experience," she told me. "I knew it would mean a lot to my daughter, but I didn't realize how significant it would be for me."

As Jean spoke, I remembered the day of her visit well. She had watched Anna and gently uttered the meditations and prayers her daughter had prepared for the women attending her immersion. Jean had been overwhelmed by the beauty of the ritual. Each woman had added her own blessings for Anna and Jean had concluded the sharing by declaring, "We are all joined as women in the family of Judaism." Anna had then entered the waters.

Jean made known her observations, "I knew then that my daughter was ready to stand under the *chuppah*."

As we admired the picture albums, I thought Anna's wedding photos were beautiful. Growing up Orthodox but unobservant in South Africa, Jean had never found a congregation in the United States where she could truly call home. She still describes our mikveh as her sanctuary. I was brimming with joy knowing Jean's presence at her daughter's wedding mikveh brought her closer to her Judaism and her Jewish past. ✐

Make me a Sanctuary so that I might dwell in it.
Exodus 25:8

Sara

*M*y mikveh experience was incredible. I learned about the mikveh from a Jewish course I took in college and ever since held the idea in the back of my mind for when I would get married. As the time drew closer to my wedding, I started investigating my options and landed upon The Mikveh at Temple Beth Hillel-Beth El.

Remembering some of the details from the course I took in college, I was a bit worried that I was signing up for something that would be too religious since the only mikveh I had ever seen was run by Orthodox Jews. However, after meeting Lori and reviewing the readings she had provided, I discovered I could create my own ritual that would feel more spiritual than overly stringent. The pre-mikveh readings Lori had chosen for me related to themes about feminism and Judaism with a modern approach.

At last the time came for my mikveh ritual. I discovered something exceedingly primordial about being naked, surrounded by water, and chanting in Hebrew. Through the process of dunking my head and reemerging, I felt reborn. I was entering a new point in my life, a marriage. After toweling off, I excitedly sensed within myself a cleansing had taken place. I loved my mikveh experience and the symbolism it contained for me. ✑

> *May the voices of joy and gladness, of groom and bride yet be heard in the streets of Jerusalem.*
> *Jeremiah 33:10-11*

Craig

Oh man, I can't say enough good things about my mikveh experience.

Before the attendant came in to supervise my immersion, I remember sitting with my dad and father-in-law, just chatting. It was one of the main highlights of my wedding week. The advice they gave me and the immense amount of pride in their voices and faces is something I will never forget.

The experience of actually going into the mikveh, to me, was all about the tradition. The fact that I was doing something that Jews on earth have been doing for literally thousands of years, was so cool to me. It is experiences and events like these that keep me so drawn to Judaism; it's similar to participating in a Passover *Seder* or lighting Shabbat candles. These traditions connect our generations and are what being Jewish is all about. ✐

Even raging waters cannot extinguish the fires of love.

Song of Songs 2:18

Kate

*T*he mikveh was by far the most meaningful and spiritually moving moment of my entire life—both as a Jew and as a woman. From the moment I walked into the mikveh office surrounded by women who were so genuinely happy to be there and facilitate my experience, the feeling was overpowering.

Rabbi Andrea Rosenthal provided me with text-based materials and questions to think about while I was preparing. Using these questions as a guide allowed me to think about what I was doing at the mikveh and what kind of experience I wanted. Ultimately, it enabled me to think about who I was, and who I wanted to be. I was able to clearly see the pieces of my past leading me to this moment, what I was letting go of, and what I was going to gain. I was preparing to set a very clear intention, even if the intention was to have no intention.

The mikveh attendants encouraged me to take my time—to slow down and not rush. I could look at my body and see it for what it truly was and not some superficial idea of what I thought it was. I was determined to celebrate the whole of my being, to celebrate and explore myself in a way I had never felt comfortable, and to look at myself and see the beautiful and hidden me.

When I finished my preparations, I was met by Rabbi Andrea, who escorted me into the mikveh room. She provided additional pieces of text, connecting the ritual I was about to enter to the ritual Jewish women had taken part in for thousands of years. Rabbi Andrea held my robe while I walked down the steps into the mikveh waters, and I felt as though she was still holding on to who I used to be while I moved forward in becoming a new woman.

With each submersion, she recited a quote from Torah or Psalms and asked me to think of something specific related to the reading. With each plunge, she guided my awareness of feeling both incredibly connected to thousands of other brides before me while also connecting with myself in a way I had never known possible. After the last immersion, we said *Shehecheyanu* together and I climbed back out of the bath. The moment I exited the mikveh and the rabbi who facilitated my entire ritual wrapped me in a white robe, I truly felt ready to become a bride. And I suddenly understood what it meant to be a Jewish bride.

I had gone to religious school from first grade through twelfth grade and growing up, I was involved in Jewish camping and Jewish youth groups. I had worked professionally in the Jewish community. I had traveled to Israel many times. I had been a part of many Jewish life cycle events for myself, my family, and my friends. Nothing, until that moment, had ever made me feel more connected to the Jewish people or more empowered as a Jewish woman until my pre-wedding mikveh. I will forever feel gratitude to the women who created this space and experience for me, and will carry it with me forever. ✐

As face answers to face in water, so does one person's heart to another.
Proverbs 27:19

Glen

Glenn, a tall, muscular, forty-something-year-old has been coming to the mikveh several times a year since he converted to Judaism. He comes for every birthday as well as on the day before Yom Kippur each year. Even Glen's Jewish friends cannot understand this ritual; his dedication, and his conviction of what the mikveh means to him. He has tried to explain to them the power of commemorating each special occasion with the ritual and the effect it wields on his life, but unfortunately they are simply unable to comprehend it.

Eventually Glen came in to mark a totally new and special occasion: his upcoming wedding. Although his wife-to-be is Jewish, she had never experienced a mikveh immersion. However, she was eager to participate in the ritual—to put her whole self into the ceremony.

"After all," she affirmed, "Isn't this what marriage is all about? No pretense, no hiding."

Glen added, "And with our marriage, we both hope there will be many more occasions to celebrate, warranting even more trips to the mikveh."

This is the day the Holy One has made, let us rejoice and be glad in it.
Psalms 118:24

Kayla

*S*ometimes the hand of God is obviously at work, weaving in and out of our lives at various moments, creating a beautiful tapestry.

Kayla's curly red hair bounced and her hazel eyes shone while talking about her soon-to-be husband, Mike. Kayla explained it had been many years since she had been happy. Ten years earlier she had lost her husband to cancer when her daughter, Emily, was only six years old. The years since his passing had been dark years of mourning, dotted with periods of acceptance, followed by daily struggles of a single working mother.

Kayla shared that she had connected with Mike through the most unlikely of places—Google! Kayla had been waiting at the DMV for teenager Emily to take her driving test, when she discovered an email from Mike. She knew Mike was a widower with two daughters: Lily, aged twenty, and Sammy, aged twenty-four. Kayla had known them all years earlier from her job back then. They had somehow managed to Google her name to find her!

Over the next hour, Kayla, and Emily, with her earbuds planted firmly in her ears, awaited Emily's driving exam. Kayla decided to call Mike on the phone number he had messaged to her, and they began to chat. It would be the foundation of a lasting friendship and eventual romance.

Kayla had come to the mikveh to celebrate her upcoming wedding.

"I never expected I would fall in love and get married again," she admitted.

Mike's daughters, Lily and Sammy, joined with Emily to celebrate Kayla's immersion. They joked about Mike being outnumbered in the home they would build together since there would now be a distinct gender difference. Kayla confided to me she felt incredibly blessed to go from a family of two to a family of five.

"I feel awed by this relationship," she proclaimed. "I want to always feel this way." ✐

I remember what it was like to be in love when I was young.
Jeremiah 2:2

Marla

When I approached the mikveh, Lori, the Mikveh Director, cordially greeted me and my mom with such warmth that I immediately felt a sense of calm. The process of mikveh immersion had forced me to focus on the momentous next chapter of my life and the challenges and sacrifices accompanying it. The mikveh provided an opportunity for me to step away from the many distractions of the minutiae of my wedding and focus solely on what was most precious—committing to my life partner. Through spiritually cleansing, I separated myself from the past and gazed forward to my new future. At the end of the ritual, Lori beautifully sang the *Shechecheyanu*, giving me an unplanned moment to thank God for the transformation ahead.

The mikveh was a tremendously spiritual and emotional experience. Immersing myself was the perfect initiation to my wedding. I am eternally grateful for the wisdom I gained in the mikveh and it will remain imprinted on my heart forever.

May we and all Israel have a favorable omen and good fortune.
Traditional Jewish Folk Song

Joe

Visiting the mikveh was a beautiful and meaningful experience for me. I decided to visit before my wedding because I wanted a chance to reflect on this wonderful and transformative time in my life. I needed to fully experience all of what I was feeling: constant excitement, hope for the future, and thankfulness for all of the love I had been given. The days and weeks before the wedding were so hectic and overwhelming, and I craved a calm and meditative space. My visit to the mikveh gave me the opportunity to slow down and be present.

As I immersed in the transformative waters of the mikveh, what surprised me most was how powerfully I was able to connect with my feelings. I thought about the joy of beginning a new life with my soon-to-be wife, and my gratitude for my family who had supported me in life. I also felt sadness that my father, who died when I was young, would not be there to see my wedding. By taking those moments to remember him before my wedding, I felt comforted knowing he would be there with us in some way. I left the mikveh feeling peace and deep gratitude. ✑

When someone you love becomes a memory, the memory becomes a treasure.

Anonymous

Michelle

*W*hat is a mikveh?

I had never heard this term until my future husband and I entered the marriage process under the guidance of our community rabbi. Quite frankly, I was brought up in the Reform Movement and was unaware of many traditional Jewish terms and rituals. In one of our early marriage sessions, the term mikveh was introduced. My interest piqued, and I thought about it, but didn't give it serious consideration until our wedding date drew closer. The mikveh immersion, I was told, would cleanse me—spiritually and physically—creating a fresh passageway to a new chapter in my life, and allow me to embrace the tradition we would uphold with our new and—God willing—growing family.

So I had made my decision . . . I would give it a try.

Afterward, I couldn't have been more impressed and grateful for the journey I explored while inside the mikveh waters. As soon as I entered, I sensed in myself calmness. Although I don't generally consider myself a ritually observant Jew, I never had a single moment when I felt unwelcome or uncomfortable. I was instructed by the attendant to take my time inside the sacred waters. I read passages and meditations while sandwiched between my mother and best friend. In that sacred space, I became mindful of each moment. I became aware of how the prayers resonated deeply throughout my body. When I completed my three immersions, I took a few moments to be alone. I was struck by the power of the mikveh. I perceived that a surprising transformation had happened inside me and, as a result, had hurtled me toward my wedding day. ✑

Delight yourself in God and God will give you the desires of your heart.

Psalms 37:4

Becca

I had never been to a mikveh before. I did not grow up living a "halakhic" life, but I grew up in a house filled with *Yiddishkeit*. The foundations of love for Jewish ritual were always present. I was, admittedly, scared to go to the mikveh. Women in my life were told horror stories about creepy mikveh ladies. As a survivor of sexual abuse, I wanted nothing to do with a vulnerable situation where a random person would check me to see if I were really prepared enough to enter the waters. So, for most of my childhood and teenage years, I never imagined I would step foot in a mikveh.

This all changed for me when I learned the mikveh could be liberating and euphoric experience. When I began "mikveh-ing" with fellow women at my summer camp, we would jump into freezing water and sing songs about Jewish women as we dunked. In the woods of the mountains, mikveh became a place and symbol for release.

Before I got married, my partner and I went to the mikveh. We chose The Mikveh at Temple Beth Hillel-Beth El because we had heard Lori, the Mikveh Director, was amazing, and that the *shomrot*, or mikveh attendants, were gentle and non-invasive.

Sure enough, the mikveh became a place of sweetness and meaningful transformation. I brought a friend with me that first time, and we sang in harmony before, during, and after my immersions. I have continued to go back to that very mikveh for many reasons: for my own monthly cycles, for marking personal time, and for healing.

To me, the mikveh is a profoundly personal and holy place. I feel at such peace as I prepare, immerse, and leave the mikveh. Going to the mikveh slows me down, and reminds me that my body is a rhythmic, alive, and holy vessel. I love the quiet that women bring to the mikveh, the stories we exchange while there, and the peace I carry with me as I leave.

In a world of change and constant motion, the mikveh for me has become a holy center of grounded stability. The mikveh pulls me back, reminding me there is holiness to harvest, and assures me of the sacredness of my body. ✍

> *When two people relate to each other authentically*
> *and humanly, God is the electricity surging between them.*
>> *Martin Buber*

Susan

During an afternoon of collating wedding invitations, Susan's soon-to-be daughter-in-law, Shira, told her she was planning on immersing in the mikveh. Growing up, Susan had never heard the term "mikveh." As an adult, she had come to have some vague sense that it was related to being very religious. When Shira invited Susan to join her at the mikveh the week before the wedding, she felt honored, delighted, and curious, and very much looking forward to the experience.

Susan didn't have any daughters and shared with me her excitement at being able to be a mom—or at least a mother-in-law—to a woman. While Susan had been anticipating bonding with her daughter-in-law, she didn't know Shira had desired the same thing until the day of Shira's mikveh immersion. Susan was deeply touched and recognized the Jewish ritual had bonded them in a relationship with each other. Shira's mom had been invited too, along with one of Shira's sisters. Susan recalled feeling uncertain about what the ritual would entail and if she would feel out of place.

The day of the mikveh, Susan felt more relaxed than she could have imagined. She shared in a personalized thank you note to me,

> *I had no idea the mikveh would be so aesthetically pleasing as well as beautiful. I truly can't tell you enough how much I appreciated your guiding presence in facilitating such a meaningful ritual.*
>
> *Being together with women who are bonded by their mutual love for the bride and who share their hope for her future happiness and contentment was one of the most spiritual and joyous events of my life and a perfect start to a magical weekend.* ✐

Great is peace since all blessings are in it.
Leviticus Rabah 9:9

Alex

*A*lex's story is one about finding love when you least expect it. Estelle, at sixty-seven years old, was a widow of fifteen years. Alex, at sixty-eight years old, was never married. They were both avid hikers and met while on the Appalachian Trail in 2001.

Alex told me he was impressed by Estelle's endurance as a hiker. She passed him frequently on the trail, and occasionally he passed her. He recounted they would sometimes meet at the trail rest stops where there were shelters and places the hikers could stop to eat or sleep. Once or twice, they shared a meal or a snack.

Estelle told me she loved how organized and clean Alex's gear was. She liked how well prepared he was for the trail and how he liked to take care of her as well. One evening, sitting around the campfire eating s'mores, Estelle and Alex decided they would finish the trail together.

In 1997, Estelle converted to Judaism and coincidentally, Alex shared he had converted in 1995.

Alex stood at the mikveh before his wedding day and declared, "Estelle and I will be starting a new trail together as husband and wife. This time our journey begins today at the mikveh."

Alex and Estelle continued to hike together in their years to come. On their trips, they frequently stopped at lakes to swim, which always reminded them of their early mikveh experiences. ✐

It is not good for a person to be alone.
Genesis 2:18

Joy

*T*he Friday before my wedding, in the fading afternoon hours before Shabbat would begin, my mother gave me some direction on where to focus my thoughts as I began this new chapter of my life.

I recognized I was parting with my life as a single person and welcoming in a life of partnership and unity. While I could never say goodbye to my family of origin, I reflected on what it would feel like to reconfigure my priorities and assign my partner as my new primary family.

I remember feeling an overwhelming sense of excitement as I experienced the ancient tradition of water immersion – one that had been practiced by women since its inception. Coming from a family of five women, and committing to a professional life of working with women as a midwife in a rural area, I was drawn to a ritual of women for women supported by women.

My emergence from the warm waters of the mikveh mirrored the birthing process I aided each day but had never experienced myself. The embryonic-like calmness and acceptance of these sacred moments soaked into every pore of my physical and spiritual being. ✎

A human being becomes whole not in virtue of a relation to themself only but rather in virtue of an authentic relation to another human being.
Aristotle

Bruce

A local rabbi called the mikveh office one day asking if we permitted transgender folks inside the mikveh for a pre-wedding immersion. I affirmed gently that our mikveh embraced all Jews and welcomed all identities.

Several months later, a man called to make an immersion appointment for his upcoming wedding. I arranged to have a male present for the groom and on the day of the appointment, I introduced the groom to his attendant.

The groom patiently explained he had a special situation regarding his immersion experience and disclosed he was in the process of gender reassignment and had not completed the transitioning process. He mentioned the conversation I had with his rabbi several months prior and I instantly recalled the phone call. The groom also asked if he could have his fiancée join him inside the mikveh immersion room because it would make him more comfortable during the sacred ritual.

I indicated that generally one gender inside the mikveh immersion room was preferred; however, it was clear these were special circumstances. I knew this young man would feel more accepted and embraced by the love of his future bride than the support anyone of us could offer him.

Afterward, they emerged from the mikveh room together and it was clear they had spent the time preparing for the special bond that would spiritually tie them together as they moved into their wedding rituals. ✌

All beginnings require that you unlock new doors.
Rabbi Nachman of Breslov

Noa

*I*n early January 2010, a few days before my wedding in Israel, my mother, sister, and I trekked across northern Israel to an egalitarian community mikveh located in Hanaton. My choice to use their mikveh resulted from the permission this community had granted me to use their mikveh in the way I had wanted—privately, without intense bodily scrutiny, and with my mother serving as the *Balanit*, or attendant.

I was tremendously anxious during my journey to the mikveh. Realistically, I knew very little had to do with the actual immersion and a great deal had to do with the wedding rituals ahead of me. My future husband descended from Jewish Moroccan and Turkish heritages, incredibly different from my own Eastern European background, and conducted Jewish rituals and etiquette in ways I had never encountered. Also, I had family flying in to Israel from all over the world to celebrate with me and it had been unexpectedly challenging to help them all acclimate to the foreignness of Israeli culture. I recognized I wasn't anxious about my future marriage; I was anxious about all the things I had been forced to agree to for the wedding rituals that were different from what I had known, expected, or wanted.

After getting completely turned around while on the road to the mikveh, we eventually made it to Hanaton. The morning of our expedition, the sun was clouded over and the cold wind bitterly pulled at our clothes. When we arrived, we were greeted by a woman from the kibbutz who provided us with the keys to the mikveh and invited us to make ourselves comfortable. We wandered our way through the kibbutz, at last arriving at the old, rundown, freestanding building housing the mikveh.

After entering the facility, we discovered the mikveh water heater was busted. Would I still choose to use their mikveh? In my mind I had no other option; the wedding was coming up and I didn't want to risk going to a mikveh where I would feel uncomfortable. And

I knew a bride couldn't get married in Israel without first ritually immersing in the mikveh waters.

Frustrated and emotional after the difficulties prior to arriving and suddenly being told the water heater was not working on this cold January day, I thought to myself, what more could go wrong?! With tears streaming down my face, I bravely entered the frigid waters. The cold waters jolted me and images of my future flashed through my mind. During first dunk, I uttered the blessings with chattering teeth and by the second dunk, I was already feeling numb, physically and emotionally. My mind froze. All the anxieties and thoughts just stopped. I let go of everything except the cold in that moment. I dunked the final time and quickly exited the pool to the warmth of towels, a robe, and steaming hot tea provided by the mikveh facilitator.

Going into the ice cold waters reminded me that the wedding was only a small part of what I would enter; it was really a marriage awaiting me. I sensed my own intense and raw emotions about making commitments not just to my husband but also to my new life in Israel and living so far from my family. In that roller-coaster time leading up to entering the mikveh for the first time in my life, just days before becoming a wife, I was given the unusual gift of cold—freezing cold—water. A gift that allowed me to release my worries and concerns and simply be present while I immersed in sacred waters. ⟡

The most beautiful emotion we can experience
is the mysterious.
Albert Einstein

Monthly

Chapter 2

Vikki

*M*onthly mikveh immersion has been the greatest gift to myself since getting married almost fifteen years ago. At the beginning of my marriage, my mikveh night became a special evening for the two of us. My husband made a lovely dinner and we took time to celebrate being together, reflecting on the beginning of our life as a married couple.

After having children, monthly immersion became something slightly different. I was fortunate to live in an area with a newly remodeled mikveh staffed by lovely, patient women. They greeted everyone with smiles and encouraged women to take their time. There was joy to be discovered in the act of cleansing inside the spa-like preparation rooms prior to immersion. I often brought quiet music to focus my intentions and I often stopped on my way home to pick a treat to share with my husband when I arrived.

Every month, I continue to enjoy and appreciate this regular interval I have set aside to relax and luxuriate, even if it is only a few scant moments in the quiet, tranquil space of the mikveh. I have prioritized taking several minutes to reflect on the role I play in my family as wife, mother, and caretaker, as well as on my own personal life-goals and journey. Without these moments I have built into my routine like monthly immersion, I am not sure I would concentrate on my life and family in this way.

Besides the "routine" benefits of having a monthly mikveh practice, I have found immersion incredibly healing at moments of difficulty. Most recently, my husband and I lost a pregnancy of twin girls. There were not many prescribed rituals illuminating the path for finding our way out of this type of loss. I went to the mikveh shortly after stillbirthing my baby girls and found such peace in the warm water around me as I immersed. The water enveloped me and gave me strength when I felt grief so deeply I can hardly describe it. After emerging out of the water, I was stronger, and ready to move forward and begin figuring out life without my babies— babies whose arrival I had been anticipating with such joy and tenderness.

There is power in the immersion ritual. I have marked moments of divine beauty and infinite loss inside the mikveh waters. Each time I descend down the seven steps of the mikveh, I reflect with gratitude on the distance I have journeyed. When I ascend the stairs, water dripping from my dark hair and freshly renewed body, I am filled with the anticipation of what lies ahead. ✍

All journeys have a secret destination of which the traveler is unaware.
        Martin Buber

Toby

*T*oby, a petite young woman with a bright smile, long, curly brown hair, and sparkling blue eyes visits the mikveh every month after finishing her cycle to observe the laws of *Taharat Hamishpacha,* or family purity. She claims the ritual profoundly enhances her marriage and reinforces her union with her husband, inviting deeper intimacy and fortifying their desire for one another.

"I put my own twist on things," she explains patiently when I curiously ask her about her choice to immerse seven times instead of the traditional three. "It's a decision I made during the wedding ceremony. After I circled my groom seven times under the *chuppah,* or marriage canopy, I decided seven had a special significance. The bride circles the groom seven times to denote the building of a strong wall around their marriage so I decided seven immersions would build a strong bond between us. And, you know what?" she asks me smiling proudly, "It works!" ✒

> *A husband and wife are one soul, separated only through their descent to this world. When they are married, they are reunited again.*
>
> *Zohar 191a*

Betsy

Since my first immersion as a younger woman, I have dunked in all kinds of places. I have dunked in traditional *mikva'ot*, outdoor swimming pools, the ocean, and in lakes. I have dunked with friends and family and I've dunked alone. Each time I return to my immersion practice, I feel grateful for my body and its rhythmic changes. I have grown so much closer to self-acceptance and being at one with my body, being fully aware of my menstruation cycle and my needs at different stages of that cycle.

For a period of time my brachot were centered on my professional ambitions, my dreams for loved ones, and my prayers for continued connection, intimacy, and love with my partner. Now I find myself savoring each month as I begin to think about starting a family. I mark time through my monthly immersions as we begin to build up to trying to conceive.

I first began observing immersion regularly because I needed a reminder of my own individual presence in the context of my marriage and partnership. I needed a space belonging to me, a time when I was focused only on me, my Jewish self, and my soul's connection to the rest of me. I felt it vital to being able to return to my marriage as a more full and more aware individual. Over time, I have observed the relationship between my partner and me works best when we each consider ourselves as fully autonomous individuals. I do my refueling inside the warm waters of the mikveh. ∽

When a person immerses their entire being in the water of the mikveh, they leave the ground of humanity and return, for a moment, to the world of elements, in order to begin a new life of purity. Symbolically they are reborn.

Rabbi Samson Raphael Hirsch
Parashat Shemini, Leviticus 91:11-47

Terra

I often think of the insights I receive as a *shomeret*, or mikveh attendant, when I perform my role. Women are frequently vulnerable and open about their feelings during this spiritual experience and I find myself gaining a great deal of understanding of what this ritual does for them and myself.

One evening, about fifteen minutes after my arrival at the mikveh, Terra called to ask how late we would be open. She informed me she was trying her best to get out of the house, and hoped to make it over in time. About twenty minutes later, she arrived, and appeared visibly frazzled. She shared that she had a two and a half month old baby at home and that this was her first trip to the mikveh since becoming pregnant. That meant it had been almost a year since her last immersion.

Terra revealed to me how trying to leave the house was really stressful for her, and she constantly debated whether or not it was even worth coming over at all. Once she finally settled in, Terra showered and cleaned in the preparation room and when she was ready, we went into the mikveh room together.

I can't explain what compelled me to do what I did, but I offered to give her a blessing since it was her first time at the mikveh since becoming a mother. She gave me a small but honest smile and accepted. I quickly darted out of the inner mikveh chamber and back into the waiting room, grabbing Rabbi Naomi Levy's <u>Talking to God</u> on the way back to Terra. I discovered the chapter, "A Mother's Prayer After Birth," and I narrated it for her as she descended the seven sacred steps into the water:

> *Thank you, God. Thank you for seeing me through this birth. For giving me this blessed child. Help me, God. Help my body heal quickly so I can tend to my baby. Restore me to strength, God. Bless me with the wisdom to understand each*

cry, and the skill to soothe it. Infuse me with the mysterious powers of a mother's intuition. Be my guide, God; stay with me through sleepless nights, send me stamina to sustain me, never leave me. Amen.

Terra spent a few quiet moments alone in the mikveh after her immersion. When she had dressed and packed up her things, she sincerely thanked me for helping create an experience so immensely meaningful, both for my patience as well as for the special blessing I had offered. She reiterated the contrast between how she felt prior to leaving her house and her calmer emotional state in that moment. Terra marveled at the renewing experience of the mikveh and confided that it almost seemed as if the prayer I read had been dedicated specifically to her. Needless to say, this was one of the many instances in which I recognized how the parts of myself I give as a *shomeret* truly impact the immersion encounters of the women who visit. ✍

God, stay with me through sleepless nights, send me stamina to sustain me, never leave me.
      Rabbi Naomi Levy

Andi

My friend and I experienced our first mikveh immersion when each of us had faced a serious medical illness. We had gone to pray for the full healing of our bodies and for the strength to face whatever was to come. The powerful experience we shared in the sacred waters of the mikveh was one of being surrounded and held by God's boundless love. When we left that day, we left with a deep sense of knowing we could trust in life and simply be present with the path that would unfold.

The power of that first experience inspired us to make monthly visits to the mikveh. Immersion was a ritual we eagerly looked forward to every month. Accompanied by our prayers, poems, and readings from the Psalms and the Torah, we reflected back on the narrow paths of our healing journeys.

Our immersions were profoundly personal and abundantly sacred. The warmth and comfort of the warm, healing waters nurtured our hearts and souls. A source of strength, renewal, and connection to each other and ourselves grew with every passing month. While originally we came to the mikveh to pray for our own healing, we immediately discovered that our circle of prayers expanded to include both people known and unknown to us.

Our monthly visits to the mikveh enriched all our connections—to ourselves, to our loved ones, to the preciousness of life, and to the Source of All Life. ✌

To the One whose goodness renews Creation daily.
Traditional Morning Service, Yotzer Or Blessing

Hadassah

Hadassah visits the mikveh monthly, ever since her marriage a year ago. As part of her pre-wedding classes teaching about different ritual practices in Jewish family traditions, she was presented with options to immerse three times or seven times. When she first arrived, she informed me she would be dunking underwater seven times instead of the usual three. It was important to Hadassah that I know she had chosen this intentionally, so that I wouldn't be confused when she did not stop at three immersions. I thanked her for having the insight to warn me in advance and she proceeded with her immersion.

After she had dried off, dressed herself, and fixed her hair, we sat in the waiting area and chatted for a few minutes. Hadassah disclosed that during her wedding, the rabbi who married her and her husband suggested she consider making this seven immersion pattern part of her monthly practice, as a reminder of the seven times she circled her husband on her wedding day. Hadassah affirmed that she not only took his advice, but added her own tradition. Every time she immerses, she devotes a private moment to recall something she is grateful for about her husband. From the details she had shared, I assured her I believed they would have a long and happy life together.

I was awed by the way the monthly act of renewal was not only being used for Hadassah's personal enlightenment, but also as a way to cherish her husband through honoring her marriage and the memory of her wedding day. ✑

Let every lonely and incomplete soul know the wholeness
of being that comes when one finds one's love.
Rabbi Nachman of Breslov

Lanie

My first mikveh immersion experience occured before my wedding and I remember it being a dry experience and lacking in spiritual connection.

Fifteen years later, I am forty-two years old, and I now have three daughters, ages thirteen, nine, and six. I spend my waking hours on my full-time career. I am fortunate to live in a comfortable house and a warm community. My husband is a wonderful caregiver and a loving man. But life is stressful. I am often so tired that when I finally get to bed, I'm asleep before my head hits the pillow. I used to enjoy sex—the touching and caring, the getting and giving of my attention....

Suddenly, women I trust began talking of the construction of a new mikveh at Temple Beth Hillel-Beth El. I'm skeptical; will mikveh usage become yet another obligation—another thing I'm adding to my stress?

While awaiting the completion of the new mikveh, a friend convinces me to try the immersion ritual again at a nearby Orthodox mikveh. Before we enter the mikveh, my friend recites a beautiful meditation bringing heavy tears to my eyes. I sense the internal nudging of some desire for spiritual depth. But I am not Orthodox, and I feel judged in this place. Nonetheless, I keep going, hoping for more, and I don a facade as I dress the part: a long plain skirt and a modesty scarf covering my hair.

When the Beth Hillel-Beth El mikveh opens, I go . . . in jeans. The inner room is a beautiful tan color and exudes the serenity I've been craving. The mikveh attendant speaks in soothing tones and it's as through I've finally been understood. This is the support I have needed. I feel pampered all over, cared for physically, emotionally, and spiritually.

This time, when I arrive home, I feel elevated, and my husband is expectant: he has lit tea lights along the staircase, changed the linens on the bed to crisp, white sheets, and hidden massage oil inside the nightstand.

I honor my mikveh practice as a way to mark the passage of time. It is time dedicated to myself and time I devote to my relationship with my husband. ✍

A time for lovers, come to my garden.
Song of Songs 7:13

Janet

I felt happy and surprised when Janet made her appointment to come to the mikveh because it had been at least six months since I had last seen her. I first met Janet when she had arrived for her bridal visit. I remembered her visit vividly. She had been joined by her mother and sister and the three of them had laughed joyously, enjoying each other's company.

She and her husband, Ben, had determined they would observe the ritual laws of *Niddah* and *Taharat Mishpachah*. These rules require husband and wife to abstain from intimate and physical relations, including touching one another during the menstrual period and the seven days following her cycle. They were confident the monthly ritual immersion would enhance their level of intimacy and add a spiritual quality to their sacred union. Ben came from an observant Jewish home and encouraged her decision. Janet continued immersing in the mikveh for about a year and then stopped abruptly.

Six months later, Janet reappeared and explained the reason she had stopped visiting. While she was completely committed to the immersion experience and surmised it was giving them what they sought, the practicality of not touching each other, holding hands, or giving and receiving hugs was too restrictive for them. They had wisely decided to take some time off from the *Niddah* and *Taharat Mishpachah* laws to rethink their commitment to the practices.

After months of soul searching, eventually they resolved to observe the seven day abstinence period, culminating with a mikveh immersion, but they would continue to hold hands, hug, and touch whenever they needed the emotional and physical connections. They had arrived at their perfect solution to their dilemma. ᧿

Each according to their strength.

Midrash Mekhilta de Rabbi Yishmael
BaChodesh 9 on Psalms 29:4

Irene

*I*rene is forty-eight years old and the busy mother of three teenagers. Her easygoing style and athletic build reflect her personality. When not at work or tending to her family, she can be found running, biking, or doing yoga. But her favorite way to spend her time is swimming.

Irene had always loved water. Her favorite memories from her childhood are of summers spent in Ocean City, New Jersey. Her father taught her how to ride the waves by body surfing and she loved spending hours diving into the ocean, feeling as if the ocean were a living being, carrying her on its waves.

Irene often comes to the mikveh to celebrate the beginning of a new Jewish month.

"I feel embraced by the mikveh. There is something here—something much greater than me. I am not alone as I start the new month. When I float in the mikveh, I feel like I am being supported. I feel embraced by the waters."

May my heart and body always sing praises to the living God.

Traditional Shabbat Song

Raizel

The mikveh chamber is eerily silent and the lights are low. In these still, ancient waters, I focus my meditations on the month gone by. I have learned in the past few months since beginning this ritual to direct my thoughts forward, onto my husband and the soon-to-be reunion we will share. Our renewal of physical intimacy every month is exhilarating and fresh and I look forward to these visits with enthusiasm.

When I lower myself into the waters nude, my entire being necessitates complete self-honesty. Now I've entered the critical point where I reflect on the way I have conducted myself, especially toward my husband. My intentions inside this holy space are crucial to my ritual and I have a practice to immerse seven times as I recognize the relationship between my body and the acts of creation.

For each of the seven immersions, I center my focus on ways I can increase the *kedusha*, or holiness, in our relationship. I must recognize the actions I can do to continually improve myself, both as a wife and a human being. There is beauty in these Hebrew words of blessing and this warm water—a beauty I strive each month to harness completely. ✐

May this be an acceptable time for my prayer.
Psalms 69:14

Peter

Shortly before I entered into the ALEPH Rabbinic Ordination program, I thought it would be appropriate for me to enter the mikveh. I found the experience connected me with deeper parts of the majestic universe within me. I began to crave that closeness and before I knew it, I was immersing before the High Holy Days and the *Regalim*, or festivals, again finding my connections drawing deeper and deeper. It was only then that I resolved to go more often.

I was aware of the many women who had a monthly practice of immersion but this intimacy with the Divine was not limited to women. Now, I too immerse my entire being inside the warm waters of this sacred ritual once a month. *Rosh Chodesh*, or the new month, has typically been a holiday devoted to women, and so I go as close to the lunar new month as possible. If it were feasible for me to travel the hour distance to the mikveh, I would go every single day.

The Mikveh at Beth Hillel-Beth El has the perfect surroundings for my sacred practice. The inner chambers of the mikveh room are quiet, dimly lit, and I am not required to obey any limitations on my time under the waters.

When I enter the room, I have my own customs I carry out and spend the first five or ten minutes in a breathing meditation. I descend the seven steps into the mikveh waters and after each plunge, I wholeheartedly declare the Hebrew blessing. When I have satisfied my ritual requirements, I allow myself to float in the comforting warmth another five or ten minutes. After emerging from the mikveh completely, I feel a quiet connection to my Jewish brothers and sisters—men and women who have repeated this experience through the centuries. ✑

> *May we rejoice forever in the words of Your Torah*
> *and Your commandments.*
>> *Ahavah Rabah*

Audrey

I have been going to the mikveh regularly for the past five years, ever since I first came as a bride. When my husband and I first got married, I enjoyed the ritual, the anticipation, and the excitement before the ceremony. Now that we have children and many obligations, I sometimes look backwards and view the mikveh as a weighty obligation imposed only on women.

To explain why I've come to feel this way, I will share that I live in Center City, Philadelphia, where there is no mikveh closeby. I must either take an uber or drive myself twenty to thirty minutes each way, returning home well into the nighttime and missing my children's bedtimes. If I decide to drive back to my house in Center City, I face the likely potential that I will spend considerable time searching for a parking space that won't necessarily be close to my home and it's an uncomfortable feeling having to walk alone in the dark.

However, in spite of all the inconveniences, when I do make it to the mikveh, I always find it deeply meaningful. I enjoy the immersion, the clean feeling, the warm water, and chatting with the attendants who work there. It's a very private affair but I feel like I'm part of a sisterhood of women—a private club sharing an ancient ritual. I am happy both of my daughters were conceived after going to the mikveh. It's almost as if I performed the ritual for them, so they would start out with a little extra holiness, even though I didn't know them yet. ✍

Be fertile and increase and fill the earth.
Genesis 1:28

Talya

*T*his would be my first time at the mikveh since my wedding. I remembered all the hustle and bustle of my wedding preparations with my mother and sisters beside me, and now I was back at the mikveh, feeling alone and nervous. Would I remember what to do? Would I remember what to say?

When I arrived at the mikveh, I studied the checklist provided on the wall. I was reminded to clean, clip, and depolish. I showered out all the gel I used to style my hair, brushed my teeth so hard my gums bled, and carefully removed all my jewelry, tucking them into a hidden pocket in my purse.

I entered the inner chambers of the mikveh room with a white robe left out for me on the stool inside the preparation room. The attendant spoke softly to me, asking if I needed anything before I immersed. I replied I was ready to descend into the waters.

I haltingly made my way down the stairs and penetrated the glassy surface of the mikveh. I once again recalled the day I visited the mikveh before my wedding. The *shomeret* had told me then that when I was embraced by the water, it was the most opportune time for me to offer special prayers to God.

This visit, during the three dunks, I first prayed for my continued health, and then I prayed for the well-being of my husband, and during my last, I thanked God for the many blessings already in my life. Everything suddenly felt right and I couldn't recall why I had been nervous in the first place. Relieved I had come, I was now ready to return home. ✐

Let the loving couple be very happy just as You made
Your creation happy in the Garden of Eden so long ago.
5th Wedding Blessing of the Sheva Brachot

Leora

*T*here are many women who visit the mikveh to mark special occasions: a birthday, an anniversary, recovery from an illness, being diagnosed with an illness, a holiday, a long sought-after achievement, a child's upcoming marriage, a conversion, or a personal search for inner meaning. There are also those who arrive at the mikveh on a monthly basis to observe *Taharat Hamishpacha*. They attend after dark because it is the custom for modesty purposes. These monthly attendees observe the ritual of marking the cessation of the menstrual cycle in order to resume marital relations.

Leora, a young woman of twenty-six, immersed every month after her marriage to mark her optimum period of fertility. I recall one particular evening when she entered the door with a long face and her body slouched and heavy. She was far from her usual cheerful self.

Leora haltingly confided in me that for the previous six months she and her husband had been trying to conceive but had been unsuccessful.

"All my friends are either pregnant or already parents," she explained, "Some of them even have the *chutzpah* to tell me they got pregnant by accident! I hate admitting this, but I am envious and frustrated. After a complete physical examination and some blood testing, my gynecologist reassured me there were no physical concerns. She advised me to wait another two or three more months before she would agree to prescribe a fertility drug. And yet, I'm determined to have my babies the way my mother, grandmother, sisters, and aunts all had them. Because of that, I am reluctant to pursue any medical interventions."

Leora sighed from the depths of her torso and rubbed her tired eyes delicately. "Tonight I plan to stay in the mikveh a little longer than usual. I need to take some time to pray for the baby that will increase the blessings of our marriage."

She floated down the seven stairs and submerged herself

under the warm, healing waters, staying under for longer than usual. After she completed her last immersion, she departed the sacred ritual as though she had been physically and emotionally regenerated. Leora confidently announced she was certain her prayers would be answered soon. ∽

God remembered Sarah and God did as He had spoken.
Genesis 21:1

Molly

I began observing the ritual of mikveh because it was a condition of my marriage. The rabbi who conducted our ceremony only agreed to marry us as long as we promised to keep the laws of *Taharat Mishpacha*. I had known this rabbi my entire life. Since it was immensely important to me that he be the one to perform the ceremony, I found myself agreeing to the unpleasant condition.

I met with the Rabbi's wife, or *rebbetzin* as she was called, for several classes. It was part of her role in the community to explain to upcoming brides and grooms all of the laws and traditions of *Taharat Mishpachah*. The way she chose to explain mikveh rituals focused primarily on men: *Niddah* imposes an obligation on men to refrain from sexual activity, not women.

This idea really stuck with me. On the one hand, it was incredibly frustrating to know I had to visit the mikveh because of my husband's obligation. On the other hand, it made me feel both powerful and kind. I perceived that I actually held the power over the sexual activity occurring in my marriage; everything was dependant upon my actions.

Visiting the mikveh is also an act of kindness, as it empowers men to observe the mitzvot, or commandments of Judaism. I recognized it to be exceedingly progressive that during the time these laws were written, many women were treated like property. Yet the laws of mikveh respected and upheld the rights of women and decreed that both partners had obligations; the wife was compelled to immerse in the waters of the mikveh and the husband had to honor the passage of time for the ritual to take place. Most importantly, each time I observed my wifely duties, I brought merit to myself and my husband. ✐

Sometimes the most important things in life don't make sense.
Rabbi Harold Kushner

Nerit

*W*hen I first married ten years ago, I remember wanting to add the element of mikveh to my wedding preparations. I had fasted and prepared for my husband-to-be, but in our community, we had only the nearby bay to immerse and I didn't fancy dipping in such an unclean and decidedly unspiritual location. Also, my husband wasn't the type of person to indulge in "needless rituals" and even though we had discussed observing family purity practices on numerous occasions, he stubbornly refused.

When my marriage ended, I found myself in another relationship where I discussed observing family purity rituals, much to the same result as my failed marriage. Mikveh and physical separation were always elements in my Jewish practice I yearned to explore, for reasons I still have difficulty putting into coherent ideas, but I knew it was one of the few practices women could do for themselves. I craved the connectedness of the women's experience and the ritualized ebb and flow of marking time in my relationships.

It's also strangely worth noting that as a woman with a severe endocrine disorder, my menstrual cycle ruled my life in cruel and difficult ways. Yet, I believed observance of the mikveh ritual would help me forge a different kind of bond between my physical and metaphysical beings.

When I at last entered into a partnership with someone who was as deeply committed to my spiritual practice as I was, I knew the time to reapproach mikveh had arrived once again.

Entering the mikveh for the first time was a fairly anticlimactic experience. I didn't really connect with the place, although the atmosphere was pleasant and relaxing, and I didn't really feel emotionally connected to the immersion routine. I completed my dips, recited my blessings, and I was out of the water. I had fulfilled my ritual obligation and off I went, returning home to my partner.

My experience continued this way for many months.

Eventually my partner and I decided the practice of separation was very challenging and engaging in ways that made sense for us and we purchased a separate bed for me to sleep in when I was *niddah*. This meant immersion rose to a new level when I was able to experience the physical reunion with my partner after abstaining for some time. However, the actual immersion itself continued to be disconnected and foreign-feeling.

After speaking with other women and hearing unconventional stories about renewal and introspection, it occurred to me I had been doing it all "wrong" from the beginning. I slowly realized the mikveh immersions would only mean something to me if I would allow them to guide me with intention and significance.

Each visit to the mikveh, I began embracing new opportunities to center myself around the month that had passed and the month ahead. I would bring full awareness to what I had experienced, holding with compassion and forgiveness in my heart all the terrifying moments of helplessness due to my illness and the seemingly endless times I had struggled with impossible tasks. Eventually, when I emerged from the waters and up the seven steps, I began to feel like I was leaving the emotional pain and weight behind me. I became a new person every time I rose up from the mikveh. Suddenly, I found myself anticipating my immersions for many reasons, but mostly for a chance to have that moment of peace and forgiveness I found hard to give myself during any other time.

Mikveh itself has become a partner to me—a quiet and non-judgemental friend who isn't afraid to hold me in my worst moments and will still be there for me month after month. She's one of my Jewish friendships I value and appreciate the most. ∽

If you are not a better person today than you were yesterday, what need have you for tomorrow.

Rabbi Nachman of Breslov

Healing

Chapter 3

Carla

Carla shuffled slowly, spoke little, and always acted impatient or hurried. She was a difficult woman to understand and even her posture projected her standoffishness and emotional unavailability. I frequently wished I understood the reason for her indifference and always tried to be friendly, hoping one day she might share a smile or a kind word. After several years of visiting, I finally got my wish. Once she opened up, it seemed as if a dam had been unleashed and the words rushed out of her.

"I needed to heal myself—both my soul and my body—to somehow attempt to recover from the abuse I tolerated for too many years," Carla whispered in a voice heavy with unshed tears.

"The pain, humiliation, and disrespect I endured day after day made me feel worthless and unentitled to love. I could never figure out what would provoke his anger or light the fire of pure hate in his eyes. Even after I left him, it seemed impossible to move beyond the cold fear and the old echoes of his voice threatening me, berating me, and tormenting me. I did not know how to overcome the nightmare that my life had become. Even after leaving him, I was in a constant state of terror he would show up in my fragile new world."

Carla spoke with courage in her voice, despite the turmoil she described.

"I knew I had to do something to heal myself, but what? And then the thought came to me: the mikveh healing waters. The healing waters would cleanse me, and make me stronger. And they did.

"The first time I entered, three years ago, I emerged feeling renewed. Each time I return to these sacred waters, I feel a new spirit take over my soul. When I began coming here, I started valuing myself and truly knowing deep inside me I am a worthy human being—worthy of love, joy, and fulfillment." ✐

The gates of tears are never locked.
Talmud Berachot 32b

Jeffrey

*J*effrey arrived so early for his immersion appointment that he practiced his Tai Chi in the parking lot as I entered the driveway to the building.

Jeffrey had a tall stature and filled the lines and grooves of his clothing with the toned muscles of his body. He had a friendly mannerism and hailed from Arkansas. In his home town he had been involved in a Jewish spiritual group and had previously used a lake for a mikveh for his pre-marriage immersion. He described the lake as remote and pristine, as if untouched since the days of Creation. Jeffrey reverently referred to that immersion as "God's mikveh," and divulged his profound awareness of God's presence there. He revealed he had visited "God's mikveh" several times and particularly liked going in the fall when the air was cool and the water was warm.

Jeffrey arrived at our mikveh seeking strength to guide him through a difficult time in his life. After immersing in the warm waters of our mikveh, he declared, "This place is truly a pool of blessings—a place where people can give and receive blessings. What is especially different about this mikveh from "God's mikveh," is that here I am also connecting to those who have come here before me."

Jeffrey's spirit had been reinforced by the blessings of those who had immersed before him and had been touched enough to leave his own blessings in return. ⌒

For I will pour water on the thirsty land, and streams on the dry ground; I will pour out my Spirit on your offspring, and my blessing on your descendants.
Isaiah 44:3

Judy and Esther

I discovered I had a malignancy in my lung in 2015 during a routine examination by my family doctor. My husband and I didn't waste any time researching my type of cancer and the best treatment methods and recovery plans. As anyone could imagine, my convalescence consumed my every waking moment, straining my relationship with my husband, family, and close friends. I clung desperately to the courage and optimism I had offered others during times of tension and despair. I had reached the point when I needed to own that strength for myself.

The surgery did not go as expected. The complications from it left me weak, emaciated, and needing more medication than was originally planned. Once I had stabilized at home, I expended a great deal of time reflecting on the overall experience of being seriously ill. I thought about how and why I became sick and what I might have done or not done to cause my illness. My stress level had been high for what seemed like a very long time and I acknowledged I needed to find a way to create balance in my life. I needed something to anchor my spirit, and searching in vain for that anchor inflated my stress levels more.

Parallel to my illness, my best friend, Esther, was enduring a similar health challenge. Recovering from breast cancer, Esther had suffered through radiation and chemotherapy treatments. We talked and decided that once we were clearly on the right side of "The Twilight Zone," we should celebrate and immerse in the mikveh together.

We drove together to The Mikveh at Temple Beth Hillel-Beth El to meet Lori Cooper, the Mikveh Director. After she graciously welcomed us and provided a personalized tour of the mikveh, I knew our experience would be meaningful, sacred, and spiritual. The mikveh was a beautifully arranged space, revealing candle lit coves and inviting furniture. The space, humid and warm, transported my thoughts to a time when women and men immersed in living waters, thousands of years before me and the life I knew.

We were given poems, meditations, and blessings to recite and were also gently encouraged to compose something of our own to read. My sister, Ruth, who lives in Israel, joined us via FaceTime and sang to us songs of comfort from Psalms. After about a half hour of reflection, Esther and I separately entered the inviting waters. Lori instructed us on how to submerge completely and offered an intention, or *Kavanah,* for us to reflect upon before each time. Once we had successfully immersed our entire body, Lori joyfully announced "*Kasher,*" to indicate a proper immersion.

At last, we were asked if we'd like to share something of our own that was personally meaningful to us. I chose to bless my children, husband, friends and relatives, and my parents – who always remained with me in spirit – and all those who helped me through this trying time. I am ever grateful for the love and support that helped my strength and positive attitude to grow, and for this experience that brought me life and sustained me and enabled me to reach this moment. This wonderful event having moved Esther, Ruth, me – even Lori! – to shed tears will be in my heart forever.

Blessed is the Source of all in the Universe, who has given us life, sustained us, and enabled us to reach this moment.
Traditional Shehecheyanu Blessing

Rina

I felt like a ping-pong ball this past month, bouncing between the twenty-first century and the teachings and traditions of my foremothers. Finally ending my civil divorce after several years of dealing with the American court system, I knew the saga of the dissolution of my marriage was not at its end. Being steeped in Jewish tradition, I knew I wanted a *get*, or a Jewish divorce document, which I was able to obtain less than three weeks later. I've always been in awe of the sages and, although I haven't always understood or agreed with everything they taught, there were certain things I would never question. With my familial connections to Israel, I wanted to leave all my options completely open. Hence, the decision to pursue an Orthodox *get*.

When I first spoke to Lori about coming to the mikveh after receiving my *get*, she suggested I begin by looking through the mikveh website. Lori explained she would provide me with some readings and *kavanot* and also suggested I bring a journal so I could record what I was feeling. I did some research on my own and was struck by one woman's blog in which she expressed the desire to recite the bracha *"Matir Asurim"* upon receiving her *get*. In English the meaning is, "Blessed is God who frees us from that which binds us."

When I shared my discovery with Lori, she left a siddur among the books and papers for me to peruse. I contemplated the texts while sitting in my fuzzy robe in the mikveh room before my immersion. Lori asked me to consider which part of the ritual I would want to recite that blessing. After spending some time by myself in the room and with Lori, I decided *"Matir Asurim"* was what I would recite before descending into the mikveh. I wanted to leave my marriage behind with the chains and yoke accompanying so much of it. As I entered the water, I felt the fusion of the twenty-first century and the teachings and traditions of my foremothers. I was now ready to begin again. ✌

I try to maintain hope, or at least the memory of hope,
when I am consumed with fear and despair.

Paul Cowan

Sherrie

Sherrie's short dark hair and square jaw made her appear intense to me when I first met her ten years earlier. At the time, she had been vocal about her opposition to the building of our mikveh. She didn't believe a Conservative synagogue should house a community mikveh.

Sherrie had been working as an attorney for close to thirty years; it was a high-powered job requiring a lot of traveling. She found herself laid off one day during the 2008 financial crisis and was devastated. Usually a successful and self-assured woman, she now had to redefine her future. Perhaps going to the mikveh would start her on that path.

On the day of her immersion, Sherrie looked different from what I had remembered. Since I had always seen her in a classy business suit, she seemed out of place in casual clothing. And the toughness in her personality seemed to have softened.

After her immersion, I received a letter from Sherrie.

> *A weight was lifted and I can begin the next step in my journey. I'm looking forward to the challenge with eager anticipation, rather than uneasy trepidation. I needed prayers and words of inspiration from the mikveh to take the leap from what was to what is, and what the future can be.*

Later, a mutual friend shared that Sherrie had begun teaching at a local law school. Although her salary had changed and the elite reputation was gone, she was loved by her students and appeared to have found her true calling. ✍

> *"For I know the plans I have for you," says God. "They are plans for good and not for disaster, to give you a future and a hope."*
> *Jeremiah 29:11*

Naomi

Naomi was a tiny and painfully shy woman. She rarely appeared in large groups and preferred to spend her time with her husband, Norman. Naomi and Norm had married right out of college and had raised two beautiful daughters. While she remained in close contact with them, they each lived in other cities and had their own lives. Norm had passed away the year before and I had recently become acquainted with Naomi outside of her relationship with Norm. Naomi had been struggling with her loneliness and privately admitted she felt isolated and unable to reach out for support to lift her above her intense grief.

I was surprised when she expressed interest in immersing in the mikveh to mark Norm's first *Yahrzeit*, or anniversary of death. Naomi was not from a traditional background and was not the type of person to leave her comfort zone.

After she immersed, she said to me with tears in her eyes, "It has been so long since I last felt embraced by anyone. These waters held me and embraced me and I feel ready to face moving on."

Recalling her words even now gives me chills. It was one of those special moments when the mikveh worked exactly as it was intended. Witnessing Naomi's immersion made me grateful for my husband—made me grateful I could still be embraced. Nothing compares to the embrace of a spouse—not even the embrace of a child, friend, or other family member.

While Naomi surely had other people to embrace, no other embrace filled that void for her. The embrace of the mikveh waters became the closest thing to the embrace of her spouse. I was reminded of how God is often described as a lover or spouse to the Jewish people. In a sense, Naomi really experienced the loving embrace of God when she immersed in the water. ✍

The left hand is under my head and the right arm embraces me.

Song of Songs 2:6

Sharon

Sharon's veins showed through her pale, thin skin. She was noticeably bruised by the many blood tests she had endured. Recently diagnosed with pancreatic cancer, Sharon knew she did not have long to live. What does one say to someone who she knows will die soon? Sharon made it easy.

When she saw me, she entreated, "Please just pray for me that I will live life fully and go without too much suffering."

After that, whenever I saw her, I would say something to her like, "I hope you have been living a full life."

I first met Sharon many years before when she had visited the mikveh to convert her recently adopted child. The welcoming of a new soul to the Jewish people created overwhelming joy for the child's parents. The waters of the mikveh were full of life and love as her new little girl became a Jew.

Now, I watched as Sharon sat on the bench inside the mikveh room and read for awhile. When she immersed, I sang a prayer to her about the angels surrounding and protecting us each night when we sleep.

Sharon continued to come back to the mikveh every month to immerse. When she no longer had the strength to immerse, she would sit in a robe on the steps of the mikveh with her feet in the water. When her cancer advanced to the final stages, she was transferred to hospice care. The change was somewhat of a relief for her since she would have fewer medical procedures. When she was no longer able to visit the mikveh, I would visit her in her home. We would sit quietly outside her home by her koi pond.

A year after her diagnosis, she finally passed away. At her *shiva,* the period of mourning observed by the deceased's family, I was asked by her husband to sing *"B'shem HaShem."* In English, the song translated to "In the Name of the Holy Name," and it was the song I used to sing to Sharon about the angels reminding us we are never truly alone.

Sometimes I think about Sharon and tears pool in my eyes. Despite the many sad occasions when I sat beside her at the mikveh, I know the mikveh helped her with her transition to new life—to a life awaiting her soul beyond this world. When I thought of her body being washed for *Tahara*, the Jewish ritual purification of the body of the deceased, I was reminded that water has always been used in our tradition to usher the soul through transition.

I choose to think that despite all of her suffering, the purity of the mikveh waters was a gentle companion to Sharon as she found herself facing the ultimate purification of soul when she passed. ༄

God will take us back in love, God will cover up our iniquities and dunk your sins into the depths of the sea.
Micah 7:19

Jill

Sima was a regular at the mikveh. (See her story on page 151.) She first used the mikveh on her seventy-fifth birthday. She would then come each and every birthday and to spiritually prepare for the Jewish holidays.

On one of these occasions, Sima walked out of the mikveh office and turned her head, calling, "By the way, as always, I've left a few of the 'blessings' I've been fortunate to receive in my life inside the mikveh for your next 'customer.'"

Ten minutes later, Jill entered the mikveh waiting room. I knew Jill very well and she was the last person I ever expected to see walk through the door. Jill was highly educated, receiving her MBA from Harvard. She worked as an executive vice president in a prestigious brokerage firm and would never consider "wasting" her time at the mikveh.

Her husband, Steve, had grown up in an observant household and found a great deal of meaning from Jewish rituals. Steve had encouraged Jill to immerse in the mikveh before their marriage and to go monthly. Steve's late mother had often spoke of its healing qualities, how it had elevated her spirit, and how it had enhanced her marriage.

Jill refused to hear any of it. She stated more than once that she considered the ritual antiquated, superstitious, and even demeaning to women.

"The mikveh is for the medieval woman, who had no running water in her house and was dependent on sharing a communal bath with the other people in the *shtetl*." Jill not only had a Jacuzzi in her bathroom, but often went to a luxurious day spa to unwind and relax.

And yet, Jill conveyed an entirely different demeanor when I met her that afternoon. Gone was the "all business, all the time" attitude, secure and self-sufficient. Her posture slumped over and refusing to meet my eyes, Jill exuded vulnerability and insecurity. She quietly admitted she had decided to try the mikveh. Jill then revealed she had been suffering from serious personal hardship and recalled her late mother-in-law repeating how the mikveh had helped to lift her burdens. Before Jill entered the mikveh room, I shared Sima's gift with her.

"There are many blessings in that mikveh room. Take them. Hold on to them."

After her immersion, Jill faced me in tears. Steve had been diagnosed with a life-long disease, and Jill was terrified of what her life would become as a result of his illness. She disclosed that throughout their marriage, Jill had insisted on being independent and strong, and had prioritized her career over family. Slowly, Jill began to grasp the idea that she might need something more in her life: spiritual aid and support to sustain her during this difficult and uncertain time. Steve's diagnosis rang the bells of an internal wake-up call; she needed balance in her life.

Jill sighed. "You know," she acknowledged, "a strange calm settled over me when I emerged. Perhaps the mikveh is really just a pool of blessings. This is what I've been needing all along." ∾

When I am afraid, I put my trust in you. In God, whose word I praise—in God, I trust and am not afraid.
Psalms 56:4-5

Shirley

Shirley's identity was built around her experience as a child of Holocaust survivors and she attended regular discussion groups for children of survivors. Shirley found it particularly odd when some of the survivors refused to talk about their experiences with their children while others couldn't stop talking about them. Shirley noticed her parents fell fully into the second category.

Every time Shirley visited the mikveh, she arrived with a special intent. She always brought special items into the mikveh with her and today she brought a giant bag to the mikveh, lugging it into the room. In a comedic scene, Shirley removed several large framed pictures out of her bag. Mimicking the scene in Mary Poppins, she continued to remove items that couldn't possibly have fit inside her small bag and lined them up on the floor on top of a beautiful piece of fabric.

"Who are all these people?" I mused out loud. She explained the photos represented her family—all deceased.

"Here are my mother and father, my grandmother and grandfather who perished in the Holocaust, my other set of grandparents, and my great-grandparents. They are always with me, and I carry them wherever I go. Today I wanted to share my mikveh immersion experience with them. They continually weigh heavily on me and at times I'm burdened by their absence. Perhaps today my load will lighten if they will remain with me as I immerse."

When leaving the mikveh, Shirley noted, "I feel lighter yet more connected to them now that we have shared this memory."

Later that year, Shirley spoke as a guest at our annual Holocaust Memorial program. She shared how the mikveh had helped her integrate her memories into hope. ✺

Cast your burden upon God, and God shall sustain you.
Psalms 55:23

Abigail

*A*bigail had lived a tough life. She had been adopted out of the foster care system into a Jewish home with her two brothers and one sister when they were young children. However, her adoptive parents later divorced and Abigail would never have the opportunity to celebrate becoming a Bat Mitzvah, the special occasion marking adulthood in the Jewish community. Her own Jewish identity shifted significantly after that event and it was a privilege she often felt she had been denied.

This morning I had received a call from Abigail who wanted to schedule a time for immersion. The previous visit had been several months prior and commemorated her receiving of her Jewish divorce document, her *get*. Abigail confessed that receiving her *get* was one of the most transformative moments in her life, despite the troubles and heartaches she had endured during her childhood. The mikveh waters provided her with a Jewish ritualistic container to hold the complex and painful emotions of that separation. In her mind, her immersion had signified the beginning of a new interval in her life.

Now Abigail prepared to celebrate her becoming a Bat Mitzvah during the coming Shabbat. She also shared she had recently purchased a new home to help her re-establish her personal identity and strengthen her self-confidence. She believed with certainty the mikveh was the most influential place to sanctify these momentous occasions in her life.

This time, Abigail knew, she would be departing the womb of the mikveh waters as a new and truly reborn woman. ◦

A Song of Ascents. I lift up my eyes to the hills. From where does my help come? My help comes from God, who made heaven and earth.

Psalms 121:1

Lynda

*L*ynda was a healer. She was a physical therapist for children with disabilities, most often cerebral palsy. She took great joy in working with children and loved to watch them grow and improve. She was close to the families she worked with and even once joined a child and his family at a hospital many states away for specialized testing, managing to combine her personal vacation with her work.

Therefore, when Lynda was diagnosed with breast cancer, she was shattered. She was responsible for caring for her own aging mother, was recently divorced, and was startlingly overwhelmed by the responsibilities of her cancer. As a result, her condition often exhausted her so much that she could not visit her patients. It had been the one energizing factor in her life.

She visited the mikveh directly after her breast cancer surgery and wanted to use it before beginning her chemotherapy treatment. After Lynda's immersion, she shared her experience.

"This has been a very special day for me," she said. "It was meaningful to use the mikveh in such a non-traditional way. It helps me see that Judaism can truly grow and adapt to new eras." She also shared she felt ready to face her troubles head on.

She called me a few days later and added, "I feel like I have so much more energy now to deal with everyday activities. I was able to accomplish so much after my appointment. I hope this feeling will remain with me for awhile."

I reassured her that when her energy got low, we could give her a refill at the mikveh. I could hear her smile through the phone. ✑

Please God, please God, heal her.
Numbers 12:13

Joan

*J*oan and Lawrence met as children in middle school, fell in love as high school sweethearts, and married shortly after graduation. He proposed to Joan on their graduation day, and they married the following winter. Lawrence was known to all his friends and family as "Babe" and "Joan and Babe" were spoken together as if they were one person—a phrase in conversation. Babe and Joan's marriage had been idyllic and loving, and Joan had spent her entire life with Babe in it.

At the age of fifty-one, Joan's recent widowhood drew her back to exploring her wedding album. She paused on each page, running her fingers slowly over the smooth images, remembering the bridesmaids dresses in the color of red winter berries, matching her bouquet.

Today is February second. It had been two years since her Babe died. February second would have been their thirtieth wedding anniversary.

"His death has paralyzed me," Joan admitted. "I even lost my job. I have trouble getting out of bed. I cry all the time. I want to move beyond this. I want to remember our times of joy together, not just the pain. I want to move into a new state of mind by taking those sacred stairs down into the mikveh."

When Joan considered herself ready to depart the mikveh, I gifted her a Book of Psalms in hope it would comfort her as she journeyed through the difficult month of February. Joan and Babe's honeymoon had lasted through Valentine's Day, and Joan anxiously dreaded the coming weeks.

She gratefully took the book, thanking me, and affirmed, "This is a beautiful book. I will spend time exploring these pages instead of crying over my wedding album. I will replace joy in the future for dwelling on my past." ✧

Hear, O God, and be merciful to me; O God, be my help. You turned my wailing into dancing; you removed my sackcloth and clothed me with joy, that my heart may sing to you and not be silent. O God my God, I will give you thanks forever.

Psalms 30:11-13

David

avid made an appointment for the mikveh and arrived with his son. Although in his mid-seventies, David acted far older; the bones of his arms and chest stood in stark contrast to the fit of his clothing, his movements were sluggish, and his hands shook with such intensity he had a difficult time holding items steadily.

"How are you feeling today?" I asked him, concerned about his physical state.

"Lousy," he replied with little hesitation. "Can I use that word here? I'm just returning from the oncologist."

"I'm so sorry to hear that," I told him truthfully. It was clear his health was quickly failing him. "I sincerely hope you'll feel better when you leave these healing waters. Is there anything special you hope to get out of your mikveh immersion? Something to keep in mind while you're in the water?"

David answered with a steadiness I had not thought he was capable of. "I want to feel calm and soothed in the waters—feelings I know I can only get from Him."

David, his son, and the *shomer*, or male attendant, went into the inner mikveh chamber, slowly assisting David as he took each careful step. He lowered himself awkwardly down each stair of the mikveh, grasping the railing with desperation. The *shomer* explained to him that once David dipped into the warm waters he would feel weightless.

After thirty minutes, the *shomer* came out to join me in the waiting room. I was curious about what was happening inside and how David was faring during his visit in his fragile state of health. The *shomer* revealed David had already immersed three times and then had requested to remain in the water a little longer by himself. Forty-five minutes later, David and his son joined us in the mikveh waiting room.

"How do you feel, David?" I inquired.

"I feel a deep sense of relief. I could have easily stayed in the water another day and a half. I was meditating and releasing my fears and concerns. I feel like a new person. I feel renewed." A glow had enveloped his features and David emanated tranquility.

I marveled at the sudden change in him. "Have you ever felt this way before?"

"Yes, once, when I made amends to my son many years ago," he responded. "A freeing of the spirit, knowing that all was in His hands."

I learned several months later David had passed away surrounded by his loving family and was finally at peace. ⌒

Strengthen yourselves, and God will give your heart courage, all of you who hope in God.
Psalms 31:25

Barbara

*A*fter one year of marriage, Tom and I divorced.

His behavior toward me changed abruptly. Where before in our marriage he had been sweet, kind, and supportive, he suddenly and with no warning or provocation, started shouting at me and calling me stupid, clumsy, dense, and ugly. He ridiculed me in front of our friends and I would retreat into silence.

I tried hard to please him; I prepared food he liked, ordered a subscription to his favorite magazine, and bought tickets for sporting events. Nothing worked. Then, one evening he came home enraged at something that had happened at work. He blamed me for phoning him during the day and ridiculing him in front of his co-workers. When I tried to answer, he pushed me against a wall and called out profanities. He slammed the door as he left the house and did not return until early the next morning.

I was scared. I did not know where to turn.

I went to a marriage counselor hoping she would recommend to me how to make our marriage better. In the end, I realized the most important thing I learned from her was that no one should tolerate such abusive behavior, and that if I stayed around, he had no incentive to change. I knew it was time for me to leave our marriage.

I felt alone, helpless, and in pain. I carried feelings of guilt and embarrassment. My friend mentioned there was a community mikveh being used for healing along with other traditional uses. She suggested I speak to the director who could talk to me about the ritual and how it might be helpful during this difficult time. I gave her a call.

She spent time telling me about the mikveh and how I might find the experience calming. She explained how to prepare physically and mentally and what to expect.

I went to the mikveh and found the whole thing to be utterly transformational. Standing in the waters, I did not feel alone. I hadn't felt like that in a long time. My pain seemed to lessen a bit. This was my first time at the mikveh but I knew it would not be my last. ⌁

Heal my heart, God. Fill me with strength to gather up all the broken pieces, and begin again.
Rabbi Naomi Levy

Deborah

Deborah's dark curls and large, expressive eyes always grabbed my attention when I saw her. Her reasons for visiting were similar to other Jewish women: to immerse monthly to mark the transition of her menstrual cycle and to ritually bathe in order to resume intimacy with her husband after a period of abstinence. During Deborah's visits, she would often share with me her private *kavanot,* or intentions, she used to concentrate while immersing.

The month following a difficult argument with her mother, she spoke the *kavana*, "Dear God, I pray for wholeness and peace. Please grant me a month of serenity."

Another month after she was compelled to choose between two similar job opportunities, she prayed, "Please God, let me know the path I should follow."

Several years passed before I saw Deborah again. She expressed sadness and regret that her marriage of three years had ended and she and her husband were divorcing. Deborah requested an appointment to visit the mikveh after she was to receive her *get*.

The day of her divorce ceremony, Deborah arrived with bloodshot eyes and dark, puffy circles underneath. She sat alone in the mikveh chamber, lights on low, as she lamented with meditations from the Bible and wept while singing Hebrew songs with special meanings to her.

With a mournful tone, Deborah sang the words, *"Kol haolam kulo, gesher tzar me'od,"* which meant, "the world is but a narrow bridge. The important thing is not to be afraid."

After her immersion, she confided in me, "A part of me is dying and yet another part of me is being reborn...." ✑

God is my light and my salvation; Whom shall I fear?
God is the strength of my life; Of whom shall I be afraid?
Psalms 27:1

Hanna

y First Mikveh

In this moment I recognize there is within me a perfect self.
A self that is strong,
Unlimited,
Huge,
In peace,
Serene,
Calm,
And Happy.
I do lot look back.
I extend my vision to love,
Good health for myself,
Sandy,
and all others.
I step into my strength to make me new.
I am not in a state of thinking,
But in a state of being.
It is pure consciousness—
Magnificence!
This state of One-ness.
I want to get in touch with who I truly am,
The part of me which is eternal,
Infinite,
and encompasses the Whole. ✐

Shema Yisrael
Adonai Eloheinu
Adonai Echad!

> *Listen, people of Israel, our God is One God!*
> *Deuteronomy 6:4*

Daniella

*I*n 2012, my husband, Mort, lost his son, Steven, to esophageal cancer.

Six days after Steven died, Mort was diagnosed with irreversible kidney failure. Two and a half years of dialysis brought us closer. We were a team. He never complained about his health and appreciated my advocacy, support, and protection.

Mort's illness and subsequent death took a toll on my emotional and physical resilience. I searched for a way to raise my spirit and heal my soul.

When I attended services, I became closer to Lori Cooper, the Mikveh Director. I told her I was struggling for a meaningful life without Mort. There was a definite void in my life which I was anxious to fill.

I knew of the mikveh ritual, but I just never thought it was for me. I was not getting married or converting to Judaism. But with a book of Psalms in one hand and a book of wisdom by Rebbe Nachman of Breslov in the other, I entered the serene, transforming space of the mikveh.

Lori was there, waiting for me, with a gentle smile and a warm hug. She wrapped me in a fluffy white bride's robe and then escorted me to a bench beside the mikveh waters. I read, relaxed, and enjoyed the sweet voice of Lori singing to me.

The immersion into the water launched a catharsis of emotion I was unprepared for and I emerged from the transformational experience with a new spirit of survival and personal fortitude. ☙

Help us to return to You and renew our days as of old.
Book of Lamentations 5:21

Jamie

After the conclusion of Shabbat one cold winter's evening in 2002, our congregation held its annual "Torathon," an evening of intensive adult Jewish learning.

I chose to attend a class on the subject of mikveh given by the rabbi's wife, or *Rebbetzin* as she was called. She began by providing a brief history of its traditional uses as practiced by observant Jewish women. My familiarity with the subject had ended there. The *rebbetzin* then continued by announcing our Conservative shul had built a community mikveh and described her vision for contemporary purposes extending beyond traditional ritual. Examples she gave utilized the mikveh for healing and the celebration of milestones or life cycle events.

I can vividly recall my tour that evening around the mikveh—the resonance of peace reflected by the soft lights of the still waters of the sacred pool, the sensation of warmth in the beautiful stonework containing it, and the tranquility floating gently in the air as it filled each of the the rooms with something undefined yet expectant.

I knew even before the class had ended that I needed to find a way to experience the mikveh for myself. I reflected on everything transpiring in my life at that time. I couldn't discern any external markers of a need for healing nor was I approaching any milestone events.

However, it was still a time of multiple challenges occurring within my family. I continued to spend a great deal of time reflecting inwardly and eventually realized I had emotionally transitioned to a place in which I had stopped reacting to situations or managing them as if I owned them. It unexpectedly dawned on me that I was on the cusp of letting go of my self-imposed responsibilities. I was reconstructing my inner landscape.

I then knew I was ready to immerse in the mikveh, marking my new intrapersonal passage. Inside those transformational waters, I emotionally and physically gifted myself precious space and time. ✑

You are wherever your thoughts are. Make sure your thoughts are where you want to be

Rabbi Nachman of Breslov

Helen

*H*elen grew up as the daughter of Holocaust survivors. She was deeply affected by the experience in part because her mother struggled with depression, unable to shake the horrific memories haunting her. Being with Helen was a constant reminder of our tragic Jewish past.

While externally she appeared as a short-haired but well-coiffed blonde, and an upper-class suburbanite decked out in diamonds and fashionable clothing, there was a stormy darkness hidden beneath. Helen's conversations inevitably always turned toward the Holocaust; her devotion to Judaism was fueled by her desire to deprive Hitler of a posthumous victory, and her interest in Jewish education centered on the need to ensure our youth understood the meaning of "never again." Even though Helen's observance of Jewish holidays was impeccable, her most meticulous preparations were saved for the community *Yom HaShoah*, or Holocaust, memorial vigil each year. Helen made certain there were volunteers to read names of the deceased aloud for hours on end. Logically it followed that Helen's connection with the mikveh would also be related to her experience as a daughter of survivors.

Helen arrived at the mikveh on a Thursday afternoon accompanied by two rabbis. She explained to us that there were spirits of several women who had experienced the Holocaust who would be "accompanying" her into the mikveh.

The first, her Aunt Ruth, had been forced to appraise art for the Nazis in Vienna and was eventually killed by them. The second, her Aunt Ellen, arrived in America after the Second World War and developed into a popular Abstract Expressionist artist and a skillful nurse, but was later killed in a plane crash. The third spirit joining her during her immersion was her grandmother, a secular Jew. She had embraced life even after her belongings, including priceless pieces of art, were stolen by the Nazis. And she had remarkably kept faith in humanity even after most of her family perished in the concentration camps.

Lastly, Helen's own late mother would be present for the ritual. Helen explained how her mother had struggled with depression for as long as Helen could remember. Her mother often shared her family's tragic stories with her. Helen said she gave her a Hebrew name before she passed away – the name *Tikvah*, hope. Helen knew there was a path beyond the stories of destruction she recalled from her youth.

Helen knew immersing in the mikveh was the first step in her journey toward hope. ✐

> *God gives strength to the weary and increases the power of the weak. Even youths grow tired and weary, and young men stumble and fall; but those who hope in God will renew their strength. They will soar on wings like eagles; they will run and not grow weary, they will walk and not be faint.*
> *Isaiah 40:20-31*

Diane

Diane's persona was outgoing, and take-charge; directly opposite of the tight blonde curls lining her petite face and her slender frame. Understandably, many people with a cancer diagnosis become fearful and retreat from friends, it was apparent to everyone Diane wasn't going to let her health prevent her from enjoying the kind of life she wanted. She made her own mikveh appointment, brought several of her closest friends, and arrived in good spirits. Even now, years later, I still feel amazed by the courage people like Diane show in the face of illness.

Diane was a breast cancer survivor and had persevered through a difficult year of chemotherapy. She and her friends recited meditations and poems, some of which I had provided to them and others which she herself had brought.

At last, when the serenity of the moment had penetrated the jovial atmosphere, Diane submerged her wearied form into the mikveh. After long moments of deep breathing, she plunged below the surface of the waters, discovering a place outside of ordinary time—a new world unfolding in the ripples of the natural rain waters. After springing up from the mikveh, her quiet prayers and blessings uttered within her heart, she returned to the loving embrace of her friends. Determination gleamed in her eyes as she swallowed her first tamoxifen pill, a treatment she would take daily for the next five years of her life.

Diane revealed to me, "I needed to let go of my anxiety about this next step in my treatment. My friends held me in a safe space in order to encourage and facilitate that process for me. I am embarking on a new phase in my life, and that's what the mikveh is all about—transition." ✐

O my God, I cried out to You, and You have healed me.
Psalms 30:3

Sam

Sam was a young, tall, and lean man with a short buzz haircut and serious blue eyes. He came to the mikveh before Yom Kippur with his father. They both had looked forward to the opportunity to immerse.

Sam came to the mikveh weighed down by images of war. He was home on military leave from Israel where he was serving in the IDF. As a soldier, he was required to endure experiences more ghastly than he thought he'd signed up for—more horrific than he could have imagined.

Serving in Gaza during Operation Protective Edge, he and his fellow soldiers were caught in enemy crossfire. There he had witnessed a gruesome scene which refused to leave his consciousness: the death of a six-year-old boy. As Sam replayed that moment over and over in his head, he recalled the boy who had been caught in the crossfire of war by a bullet which might have been aimed at Sam. The sight of the small boy dead on the pavement, the sound of the child's grandmother wailing as she hovered over his little body, and the vision of two soldiers falling onto their knees as they beheld the true horrors of war, were all excruciatingly painful to remember. The scene continued to play in his mind, without control, day and night.

His father had hoped the waters of the mikveh might bring some relief to his son's suffering. Sam acknowledged he had found the water pleasant and soothing. Sam had initially hoped the experience would help him move in the direction of healing, but he understood now that it had been overly optimistic. Jewish ritual could be powerful but was not magic and couldn't replace the hard work needed to overcome the terrible scene he had witnessed.

In two weeks, Sam's visit would come to an end. He would return to Israel, perhaps once more surrounded by scenes of violence, and he would certainly have to live with the images replaying in his mind—the harsh sights and sounds of war. ✑

Signs of your nearness offer me support and comfort. When faced with fear, your love flows over me and sustains me.

Psalms 23 - Interpretation by Sheryl Lewart

Ellie and Jodi

A narrow wooden bench sits inside the room of our mikveh. Like a bench beside a mediation bond, our visitors frequently adopt positions on it as they reflect before their immersions. The bench also provides a comfortable landing place for friends or family to relax as they accompany immersants.

On a rainy Monday afternoon, tears of mourning dropped softly onto our meditation bench. A mother and her daughter had come to the mikveh to mark the *yahrtzeit* of Jonah, their son/brother. Jonah died after a long and painful battle with cancer and they continued suffering the absence of his witty sense of humor and generous heart. While neither of the women had ever visited a mikveh before, the longing for Jewish ritual was part of their collective soul; they both came to it naturally.

Inside the mikveh room, the tranquility of the space was occasionally punctuated by whispered voices and quiet sobs. Ellie, the mother, and Jodi, the daughter, nestled beside each other on the bench while reading words of healing, encouragement, and strength. When I entered to facilitate the immersion, Ellie submerged first, and after plunging three times with tear filled eyes, she recited the "*Shehecheyanu,*" the prayer of praise to God.

Jodi immersed three times and when she reached the moment to chant the "*Shehechiyanu,*" the words faded off as her voice broke. Sobbing, she pleaded, "How can I say that blessing? I can't thank God; my heart is broken."

Ellie answered her gently, her own voice struggling to hold back her tears. "You *must* thank God because *you* have reached this day. You are here with me and alive. We are fortunate we have each other; your brother is gone, but we are here together."

Ellie's support of her daughter highlighted the comfort she continually discovered in her own life, despite her loss. Ellie endured the worst kind of loss with fortitude and her steadfastness was nothing short of heroic. ✑

> *O loving God, help me discover and uncover all that is good,*
> *all that is positive in the world.*
> *Rabbi Nachman of Breslov*

Conversion

Chapter 4

Greg

Greg had been studying about Judaism for thirty years, ever since he met Nancy, his wife.

"I was completely captivated by its intellectual components," Greg acknowledged to me. "I was intrigued by the notion that this religion was able to survive over so many thousands of years, against all odds. I was fascinated as well in how Judaism appeared so dependent on rational inquiry but was still able to connect spiritually with the divine. I had no intention of converting to Judaism when I first met Nancy. My interests in Judaism were purely intellectual and philosophical."

Greg did promise Nancy they would raise their children as Jews. He committed to making every effort to support her in her determination to create a Jewish home celebrating all the holidays – from the weekly Shabbat observance to the annual High Holidays. And indeed, he had kept his promise.

Greg worked for a large technology company and had an international reputation as a leader in his field. Despite his high profile job and frequent domestic and international work trips, he had managed to be home every week to celebrate Shabbat with his family. Through the years, he had habitually studied Judaism, despite his engagements in teaching and research.

Several years ago, Greg was diagnosed with ALS, a degenerative disease which, in its final stages, rendered a person totally dependent on others. He had not progressed quite that far but as time passed, he knew it would become more and more difficult to reach that pinacle point of conversion. Greg's interest and appreciation of Judaism had grown and deepened to the point where he was ready to convert to Judaism.

Greg declared, "All my life I toyed with the idea of conversion and now the time has come. I need to get to the mikveh while I still can. Before ALS I was a strong man, an athlete, a runner, and a swimmer. Now I'm going to need help just getting down the steps of the mikveh."

On that special day, Greg arrived with his sponsoring rabbi: someone who would help him down the steps as he entered the mikveh waters. The rabbi explained he would let go of Greg for each of the three immersions just for a moment. Greg floated in the water and felt a return of buoyancy and with it, joy. When he emerged, Greg boasted he had been able to walk up two steps at a time.

"I haven't been able to do that for a long time. I want to internalize this experience and capture this moment so I can return to it and hold it close for the rest of my life." ✍

The world is a narrow bridge, the main thing is not to be afraid.
Rabbi Nachman of Breslov

Annie

*T*hirteen-year-old Annie had been adopted as an infant and had been raised as a Jewish child. Two weeks before her Bat Mitzvah, her entire family was eager for her to undergo a ritual conversion. Traditionally when a non-Jewish child is born and the parents want to convert the child, the child is brought to the mikveh as an infant or toddler. Annie had never been immersed as a child and had developed into a tall, pretty child with a long brown braid bouncing between her shoulders. At thirteen years old, she was slender, with long arms and legs, and her dark complexion was clear. Annie was showing the first indications she would grow into an exotic and beautiful woman.

When she arrived, her smile was tentative. Annie seemed apprehensive, defensive, and acted a bit suspicious. She was not sure at all why she was at the mikveh. She arrived feeling uncertain about proceeding with this fundamental ritual of conversion.

Prior to her arrival, she had been informed anyone immersing must be naked when entering the mikveh. The reality of being naked was too embarrassing for her to talk about, even with her mother. After she arrived, when reminded she would have to remove her clothing in order to immerse in the water, Annie's demeanor completely shifted. In a split instant, the difference between theory and practice hit her hard.

"What?! Take off my clothes?! I can't do that!" She was adamant and continued to exclaim, "It's too embarrassing! I can't!"

I patiently described the process, assuring her she would have complete privacy getting into the mikveh. I promised I would keep my eyes closed as she walked in and when she dunked, I would only be checking to make sure her head and body were completely submerged.

Just as Annie was about to enter the mikveh waters, the room plunged into darkness from a local power outage. The mikveh room, whose lighting normally provided a warm and ambient feeling, had failed. It was several long moments until the emergency lights automatically sprang to life and provided just enough light for Annie to see the steps for her to descend and for me to be able to witness the immersion. Annie sighed with great relief as she dropped into the warm water.

"I guess someone up there is looking out for me," she whispered, and felt her privacy completely protected with the loss of electricity. ✐

Hope for a miracle, but don't depend on it.

Talmud Megillah 7b

Dean

*T*ammy and Dean met during graduate school. Although Dean came from an Italian Catholic background, he didn't consider himself particularly religious. Other than having some emotional attachments to holidays like Christmas, he didn't feel resistant to exploring Judaism.

After the birth of their son, Aaron, Dean realized he was ready to join the Jewish people. Having a child had changed Tammy and suddenly she seemed so intent on everything being Jewish. When it was time for Aaron's *bris,* or ritual circumcision, Dean, as the non-Jewish partner, had felt very left out and was determined to make sure he would never again feel that way as he raised his son.

As Dean studied more about Judaism, he felt it was the perfect road to being a better husband and father. He shared how committing to Judaism had given him guidance, direction, and a path on which to move forward. The mikveh was an emotional experience for him, as it symbolized turning in a new direction and leaving the old behind. When he was about to immerse for the third time, Dean said he took a deep breath and exhaled slowly.

"I went under the waters and gently rocked myself from side to side. I lost all sense of direction. Was I facing north, south, east, or west? I had no idea how deep I was and felt totally disoriented. But when I emerged, I realized I was exactly where I wanted to be. Now I feel prepared to move in the direction that is right for me." ᐦ

Show me your ways, God, teach me your paths.

Psalms 25:4

Jana

I first met Jana when she came to tour the mikveh before her big appointment. Jana was a vivacious young woman of twenty-one with short hair, big dangling earrings, and bright lipstick. She had grown up in a medium-sized town with a sizable Jewish population, and many of her adolescent friends were Jewish.

Her family was quite well-off, and she always had everything she needed as a child and young adult. But she described feeling a spiritual void throughout her youth. Her family did not identify with any religion and her parents were quite surprised when she expressed interest in Judaism. They thought it was just a phase and hoped she would eventually drop the interest. When they saw she would not, they gradually came to accept her desire for Judaism, although they never understood it.

When Jana came to the mikveh with her sponsoring rabbis, a friend, and her mother and father, she looked very different without her makeup and jewelry. That day she would immerse in the mikveh to become part of the Jewish people. She explained to me that at sixteen, after being stirred by a program on the Holocaust, she decided she wanted to learn all about Judaism. Jana observed she felt like she had been preparing all her life for her conversion immersion.

"I am really coming back to Judaism. My great-grandmother was Jewish, but her daughter, my grandmother, converted to Christianity. I am coming home! I am about to rejoin the people of Israel."

Jana mentioned she had been in Israel two weeks earlier and shared the highlights of her trip; she loved celebrating the Jewish Sabbath and visiting the Western Wall in Jerusalem.

"I was standing where others had dreamed to stand but had not been able to."

Jana had decided to take her great-grandmother's name, Hannah, for her Hebrew name, and continue along her path. As Jana celebrated with her family after the ritual, I had the sense I would see more of Jana's mother as she explored her own Jewish roots.

Then Hannah prayed and said, "My heart exults in God."
1 Samuel 2:1

Evan

*A*t three years old, and newly Jewish, Evan appeared as a spiritual adult. It is often said children are closer to God. Perhaps this is because they are closer to the experience of the womb, where according to tradition, they learn the entire Torah. And maybe, the womb-like experience of the mikveh brings out that spiritual wisdom in children who immerse.

After toddler Evan immersed in the mikveh, he took a shower while his mother, Kerri, stood nearby to help. Kerri shared with me that when she asked if she could turn off the water faucet, he exclaimed, "No, not yet! I have a little mikveh left on my foot. I need some more soap."

"I thought it was so curious," she said, "that he saw the mikveh as the living thing that it is and not just as water. He had some on his foot and needed to get it off!"

Kerri also revealed how Evan had sung while getting dressed after his immersion. She confessed, "He has an unusual knack for the appropriate, especially given that he is only three years old. Evan was singing his favorite song of the moment, which is really only one line from "*Shalom Aleichem*," that we sing to welcome the Sabbath. Over and over he sang "*Mi Melech mal'achei ham'lachim Hakadosh baruch Huuuuu!...Mimelech mal'achei...*"

As I listened to Kerri, I thought about the connection between the songs I would sing when attending an immersion and the song Evan had been singing. I often sing *B'shem HaShem*, a song referring to the angels guarding us in life. Evan was singing *Shalom Aleichem,* referring to the angels who accompany us on Shabbat.

According to the Chassidic Jewish tradition, converts to Judaism are actually born with a spark of a Jewish soul. When the convert immerses in the mikveh, the Jewish soul is fully born. Just as a baby exists in the womb, but reaches full life at birth, so, too, the convert contained a Jewish spark when born—a spark which becomes a full Jewish soul within the depths of the mikveh. Perhaps

Evan was singing about angels because just moments earlier, his Jewish soul fully emerged and he was introduced to the angels accompanying the Jewish people. ✐

In the name of Adonai
the God of Israel:
May the angel Michael be at my right,
and the angel Gabriel be at my left;
and in front of me the angel Uriel,
and behind me the angel Raphael . . .
and above my head
the Sh'khinat El, the Divine Presence.
From the bedtime "Shema" prayer

Marion

Marion had awful memories of swimming lessons as a child. Her family was wealthy and she had attended an elite, all-girls school emphasizing everything from education to academics to etiquette to sports. She remembered shivering by the pool and not wanting to jump in the cold, chlorinated water. Because Marion was an obedient child, she always went into the water as she was told. But she was afraid of going into the deep end, even as all the other girls practiced fancy synchronized swimming and then frolicked at summer pool parties with boys from the neighboring all-boys prep school.

Marion just never fit in. Not with the other girls, not with the prep-school crowd, and not with her upper-class family and their social groups. It was only after attending Barnard College that she was exposed to all kinds of people, and discovered Judaism. Luckily, becoming Jewish didn't involve any of the activities she had been groomed to accept, such as horse-back riding, country clubbing, or Christmas crafts.

Marion watched the Jewish community from the outside, and went on to watch many other cultures from the outside as well. Majoring in anthropology, she traveled the world for her research, fascinated by traditions seeming so foreign to her. She never married or had children, but she did eventually end up back in the Philadelphia area where she was raised. Eventually, she chose Judaism at the age of sixty.

Just as she had as a child, Marion still feared water. She was not thrilled to learn about the tradition of mikveh, but her travels around the world helped her put things in perspective and made her willing to take risks. She needed something strong enough—something big enough—to help her let go of her fear of the water. The strong enough and big enough motivator for Marion was the feeling of holiness in her life.

After her immersion, she exclaimed, "I felt so safe. Thank you for not letting me get away with an improper dip! I feel like Godzilla. I feel so strong. I'm Jewish!"

Marion went on to choose the Hebrew name "Maayan" meaning "spring of water," because she had been so moved by her mikveh experience. ✐

And the sea split before them and they passed through on dry land.
>   *Nehemiah 9:11*

Rachel and Yentl

When Corrine went to Guatemala to adopt her first daughter, Ixchel, she was deeply troubled by the terrible persecution suffered by the indigenous Mayan population. Gazing at her new baby daughter, she was determined to learn about the culture of the Mayan people. With a delightful surprise, she discovered both the Torah and Mayan tradition taught time is a cycle through which all things are interconnected. Three years after adopting Ixchel, she returned to Guatemala and adopted her second daughter Xpiayok.

Corrine raised her two daughters as Jews, but struggled for years about whether she should take them through a formal conversion process.

"It is important to me that my girls know they are Jewish, but I also want them to learn the culture of their Mayan ancestors," she explained. The day they came to the mikveh, Ixchel was thirteen and Xpiayok was ten years old.

"We are nervous," Ixchel admitted to me. I could tell they did not want to be naked in front of me, so I calmed their fears by showing them the beautiful sarongs we used for modesty at the mikveh. I also demonstrated the way I would wait until they were in the pool before looking directly their way.

When they were done with their immersions, the girls insisted they were relieved and happy.

Xpiayok shared with me, "I always thought on my birthday I would feel older, and different, but I never did. Today I feel changed."

Ixchel added, "It changed my life. I felt like an eagle."

Corrine elaborated on her daughters' comments. "In the ancient Mayan culture, the eagle symbolizes inner knowledge and wisdom, two things valued by both the Mayan and the Jewish people."

Choosing Hebrew names was not difficult for the girls either. In Mayan culture, Ixchel is the jaguar goddess of midwifery and medicine and sounded the closest to the Hebrew name *"Rachel."* She then chose *"Nesher"* for a middle name, meaning "eagle" in Hebrew. Xpiayok, named for the Mayan goddess of matchmaking, chose the name *"Yentl"* from which Yenta is derived, and for a middle name *"Yocheved,"* since it sounded like Xpiayok.

Taking her daughters in her arms for a big hug, Corrine was thrilled with their immersion experiences. "I truly feel we are all interconnected," she attested, "and can learn from all peoples, for we are all of one God." ✐

We come from different places, we may take different paths but we are striving to know the same God.

Anonymous

Phyllis

*P*hyllis had been married a long time to her husband, Steve. They had two daughters, Sadie and Molly. When the time arrived for Sadie to become a Bat Mitzvah, Phyllis became increasingly uncomfortable with the fact she had never converted. Phyllis had watched as both her daughters had used the mikveh for their conversions years earlier and had always sensed this was a step she would one day take.

As a mikveh director, I consider carefully the people who come and what I want to say to them. With Phyllis, I had the thought to speak with her about joining and unifying her family into one heritage. While I did talk to Phyllis about those things, I also learned from her about the power of silence.

After Phyllis immersed, she told me, "The third dunk was the best. I felt the sensation a baby might feel inside the womb. I felt encased within the warm waters. It was like being in a big snowstorm when everything is blanketed in silence."

This was a woman carefully attuned to sound. I'd noticed for many immersions, there is often a lot of talking and singing in the mikveh. There is frequently the sharing of blessings and an expression of wishes. But sometimes the most potent sound of the mikveh is the silence.

When guests arrive at the mikveh, I still think of what I can say to them. But I also remember Phyllis, and reflect on how I can facilitate the mikveh's teaching its own Torah – through silence. ✑

To every thing there is a season, and a time to every purpose under heaven: a time to keep silence, and a time to speak.
Ecclesiastes 3:1,7

Rebecca

*M*ichael and Cindy had been married for many years before they decided to start a family. After years of trying to conceive unsuccessfully, they instead pursued adoption. They attended a regular support group sponsored by their adoption agency where clients were encouraged to attend to learn about the issues facing adoptive parents. For Michael and Cindy, waiting was an incredibly painful process. Two adoptions fell through before they received word there was a single, pregnant woman in Salt Lake City who was placing her child for adoption.

They traveled to Salt Lake City to bring home Rebecca while she was a newborn. When Rebecca was three months old, they brought her to the mikveh for her conversion, with their family rabbi of many years. It was a special moment because friends and family joined them and each person had been aware of how long Cindy and Michael had waited to adopt.

After the conversion, Cindy revealed, "I was so emotional when I carried my daughter into the mikveh. I knew I needed to slow down in order to be in the moment. It was our first step in raising our Jewish child. The mikveh was the right place to make that commitment. It all made sense. I took our daughter into the warm mikveh waters and we watched her emerge as our Jewish child." ✐

Shout for joy to God, all the earth.

Psalms 100:1

Marla

*W*hen Matt and Karen adopted Marla in the 1970's, the adoption process was far different than it is now. There were fewer specialty adoption clinics and fewer non-traditional families. Today, prospective adoptive and birth parents can choose whether they would like to take part in an open adoption; a partially open adoption, in which the birth parents have the option to have information shared when the child is an adult; or a completely closed adoption.

Back when Marla was adopted, the lines were less clear. It wasn't always certain what information would be shared nor was it clear all the information they received about the birth mother was correct. When the agency told them the birth mother had been Jewish, they'd had a sneaking suspicion the agent might have just told them what they'd desperately wanted to hear. But they were so excited to adopt the baby, they decided to take it on faith and accept all the information they were given: the mother was a healthy, Jewish college student who had become inadvertently pregnant by her boyfriend.

Marla was thirty years old when she came to the mikveh. She had recently searched for her birth mother and discovered she was not actually Jewish. Marla had been raised in Matt and Karen's Jewish home, attended a Jewish camp as a child, and had also been a teacher in a Hebrew school.

She was now preparing to get married and was told by her rabbi she needed to immerse in the mikveh to be considered Jewish according to Jewish law. The experience of being questioned about her status as a Jew had been quite upsetting to Marla. She was confused and angry.

After her immersion, Marla told her parents and the friend accompanying her, "The immersion was spiritual and felt like the right thing to do. Today wasn't a conversion for me, it was an affirmation of my Jewish identity. I plan to come back before my wedding day." ✍

The only person you are destined to become is the person you decide to be.

Ralph Waldo Emerson

Lisa

*T*hirty-two-year-old Lisa never expected to find herself at a mikveh accompanied by her parents, Michael and Jane, her boyfriend, Ben, his mother, and her two college roommates. The mikveh waiting room could barely accommodate this lively group of those in Lisa's closest support network who had come to support Lisa's conversion to Judaism. Lisa was raised in a Christian home, celebrated Christmas and Easter, and never gave Judaism much thought. Then she met Ben while in college and the two started dating. They had an abundance of commonalities, even though Ben was Jewish and Lisa wasn't.

After graduating college, they went their separate ways. Lisa moved to New York to start a career with a large public relations firm, and Ben relocated to Chicago to attend law school. They did not stay in touch and were delighted and surprised to run into each other several years later at an art exhibit in Soho, Manhattan. They went out for dinner and soon resumed their former friendship.

A year later, Ben invited Lisa to meet his family. His mother was a warm, friendly woman and made Lisa feel comfortable and welcome. The very next day, Ben proposed and Lisa accepted. She was amazed at how quickly she felt familiar and relaxed in his parents' home. His mother invited Lisa for her first Shabbat dinner and Lisa felt so comfortable with all the rituals, it was as though she had experienced them before.

She decided to do some genetic research on her background and with the combined help of a computer program, genetic testing, and a bit of family history digging, she discovered she was not a complete novice to Judaism.

Lisa's great-great-grandfather was born in Izmir, Turkey, home to a large intellectually wealthy and politically influential Jewish community. The Jews of Izmir enjoyed freedom and equality until the early part of the nineteenth century when they were accused of participating in a blood libel by the Greek community. It was at this time that Julie's great-great-grandfather, a perfume salesman, emigrated to France and eventually to Mazatlan, Mexico.

He was still a practicing Jew in Mazatlan at the time of the birth of Lisa's great-grandfather. Her great-grandfather was a practicing Sephardic Jew and moved to California in the early part of the twentieth century. Lisa's grandfather married a gentile woman, Jane, and they chose not to practice Judaism. Their daughter, Lisa's mother, did not know about her Jewish roots.

It was through Lisa's probing and decision to convert that her family's roots were unearthed. ✑

When one comes to be converted, receive them with an
open hand, so that they can come under the wings of
the Divine Presence.
      Leviticus Rabbah 2:9

Bella

Coming to the mikveh for conversion is a joyous event for most families. This conversion was different. I knew from talking to Jacob over the phone that he wasn't happy about having to convert their adopted daughter and Leslie had looked annoyed when she arrived. Baby Bella, on the other hand, was very smiley and didn't seem to notice her parents' apprehension.

Jacob and Leslie adopted Bella from China when she was just two months old. They had brought her home to their very Jewish environment, observing Shabbat, holidays, and *kashrut*, the Jewish dietary laws.

One day, they received a phone call from their rabbi who told them, "It's time to bring Bella to the mikveh."

Jacob was taken aback.

He questioned the rabbi, "Why do we need to bring her to the mikveh? We've been observing Judaism with her in our home. Why do we need to do this to our nine-month-old baby?"

They arrived reluctantly, but soon after seeing the beauty of the mikveh, their faces softened and they realized Bella, who loved water, would not mind the experience. After Jacob immersed Bella three times, he lifted her out. Jacob was overwhelmed with emotion.

He told me, "It was like watching her being born. We were not there for her birth into this world, but today we watched her birth into the Jewish world."

Leslie too was tearful. The two of them decided to celebrate her formal conversion with the giving of her Hebrew name that week during Shabbat services. ✑

We prayed for this child and God has granted us
what we asked.
    1 Samuel 1:127

Lilly

*T*hree year old Lilly came to the mikveh with her parents, Josh and Cynthia. She was terrified as she looked around the room; in spite of the fact her mother held her in a soothing, gentle embrace, Lilly looked as though she was in the middle of a nightmare. Lilly had lived a frightening past. She had been brought into foster care shortly after her birth and even for a three-year-old, change was not something to which she looked forward. She clung to her adopted mother's neck and quietly sobbed.

Cynthia, Lilly's mother, understood the panic her little girl was facing. A foster child herself, she had been placed in different foster homes growing up. Her own parents had died when she'd been very young and she grew up living with several families. She never felt like a permanent member of any one family and was always careful to behave lest she be returned like a library book.

Cynthia and Josh already had three biological children together when they decided to become foster parents. The children they fostered were usually temporary placements and it was always painful for Cynthia to have to give them back to the agency.

When Lilly arrived as a newborn, Cynthia was determined to pursue adoption. She wanted so much to make another foster child become wanted, cherished, safe, and loved. It was a draining process but Josh and Cynthia were persistent and it paid off.

They brought three-year-old Lilly to the mikveh as soon as they left the courthouse. At first Lilly was frightened; she couldn't understand the courthouse process or why she had been taken to this strange place. She looked upset when she and Cynthia first entered the mikveh. However, upon emerging, Lilly was smiling as Cynthia wiped joyful tears from her own eyes. Josh and Cynthia held Lilly tightly as they officially welcomed Lilly into their Jewish family. ✍

All of us have an angel of God calling out to us to show us the way; to blessings, to clarify and to prophetic vision.

Rabbi Naomi Levy

Margaret

*M*argaret, a blue-eyed, light-complexioned woman, was in her mid-fifties when she first came to the mikveh. She took her oath as a Christian minister at the age of twenty-two. She loved her religion and thought she would spend the rest of her life consecrated to Jesus.

Margaret taught fourth grade at the local parish school, woke up early each morning to attend mass, and initially enjoyed the predictability and consistency of her life. The routine made her feel safe and she knew she would always be protected by the church.

About twenty-five years after she took her vows, she began to question the absolute obedience which was required of her. Doubt began to erode her faith. Through her extensive reading, she'd discovered there was a whole world she had never explored. When she queried her superiors about the many obligations she was forced to take on, she felt she did not get satisfactory answers.

After deeply searching and agonizing within herself, she decided to leave the church. It had been an immensely difficult time for her. She took courses at the local university about religion and it was at this time she met a Jewish woman—a woman to whom she felt deeply attracted. They forged a strong bond and eventually decided to live together. Margaret studied Judaism and made the decision to convert.

Margaret arrived at the mikveh for her conversion ceremony and as she turned her back to me to descend the steps into the water, it was a first for both of us: for her it was immersing in the mikveh, and for me it was witnessing the immersion of a former Christian minister who had decided to embrace the Jewish faith. ✑

Prayers truly from the heart open all doors in heaven.
Rabbi Nachman of Breslov

Four Boys

S cott and Denise traveled two hours from their small town to arrive at our mikveh. They came with the only rabbi who covered the large geographic area where they lived. Most of the Jews from their small town in northeastern Pennsylvania had moved out of the area over the years, and those who had remained were intermarried and increasingly assimilated.

Unlike many of the children of local Jewish families, Scott had retained a strong sense of his Jewish identity. When he married Denise, a non-Jew, they had spoken of religion as a matter of national identity rather than ritual observance. Scott worked as an electrician and Denise answered phones at the local cable company. Scott remained connected to synagogue life and even made electrical repairs to the building at no charge.

Despite their small Jewish community and their limited involvement in the ritual aspects of Judaism, they did want their boys to become B'nei Mitzvah, sons of the commandments, and didn't question the rabbi's insistence on conversion.

The four boys – aged ten, eight, five, and four – came to the mikveh with Scott and Denise. Although Denise was not Jewish, she and Scott had agreed to raise the children as Jews. Denise seemed quite excited about the day and shared with me how converting the boys was important to her. She remarked it was similar to her feelings about having them circumcised as newborns so they could be "just like their dad."

Scott replied, "I believe you have to know where you came from to know where you are going. That is why we are all here today." ✑

As my family planted for me, so do I plant for my children.
Talmud, Tractate Ta'anit 23a

Jiwon

*J*iwon was raised Christian in Korea. She and her husband, Brian, who was Jewish, were raising their three kids within Jewish tradition. Together they witnessed a *Bet Din* formalize their children's conversion in a mikveh. Brian knew at some point in time Jiwon too would convert but had no idea when the right time would happen for her.

Growing up in a strict Korean home meant many things for Jiwon, including respecting, obeying, and honoring her parents, culture, and society. Jiwon was raised to revere her parents and not to question the faith, tradition, or tenets of the Christian religion. Her parents were not aware of her interest in Judaism and her ultimate desire to convert. She knew it would only hurt and anger them. Jiwon had not found meaning in Christianity, did not attend church, and had been living a Jewish life with her husband and children. She wanted to privately take this final step of conversion; it was her faith and personal relationship with God leading her to this point. It was a relationship she would continue to build on her own.

These were some of the thoughts reverberating inside her head as she immersed in a pool of blessings. To Jiwon, mikveh was an inner conversion. She exquisitely focused on her soul and spirit as she entered the mikveh. Not an act of defiance from her birth religion, but an act of personal transition and growth. She had found a home in the Jewish community. It was time to take on a new culture and a new way of thinking about respect—a way that encouraged questioning. And for Jiwon, this was truly liberating. ✍

Dear God, teach me to begin anew, to renew myself with all of creation.

Rabbi Nachman of Breslov

Dina

*U*pon completion of her thirty weeks of Jewish study, Dina thirsted for more involvement in Jewish life. She looked forward to becoming a full-fledged member of the Jewish community, but as the course neared its completion, she grew anxious and even apprehensive. When the course concluded, the entire class came to the mikveh to familiarize themselves with the facility and the procedure taking place on conversion day.

Dina lingered at the end of the class and divulged she was particularly anxious about the mikveh immersion itself. In my years of experience, it is normal for people to feel uncomfortable about entering the mikveh naked. The concept of standing before God without pretense and without any barriers between you and God was intimidating and daunting for many. But I observed more to Dina's anxiety.

Dina explained she had a fear of putting her head below the water as well as equally concerned about being naked during the ceremony. We spoke for a long while about her background and her fear of water. She confided in me a frightening experience that had occurred; when Dina had been a child, she'd nearly drowned in a pool. Dina asserted she was actively seeing a therapist and was working through her issues. I suggested she brainstorm with her counselor about how to navigate the mikveh experience in a way she would feel more comfortable and safe.

Dina ultimately decided to delay the ceremony from her fellow course participants and instead practiced at a public pool, experimenting with putting her head and body under the water. Her conversion would wait until she felt more confident in the water and therefore more at ease with the ritual of immersion.

Several months later, Dina finally came for her conversion and seemed more at ease and focused. I went over again the different steps of the ritual. I assured her I would turn my back completely so I would not see as she descended the steps and reemerged later. I promised I would turn around and open my eyes only when she felt comfortable. Dina was certainly nervous about the ceremony, but later the smile on her face reflected her sense of joy upon reaching this special transition moment in her new Jewish life. Dina left the mikveh beaming, thrilled to be officially counted among the people of Israel. ✐

Happy is she who dwells in Thy house....
Psalms 145:1

Shari

Shari grew up Catholic and enjoyed Confession in particular. Confession gave her the ability to unburden herself of small daily imperfections and "sins." She perceived that speaking to the priest with the partition between them was a perfect mix of closeness and privacy. While the priest could hear her voice, he could not see the expressions on her face or see her tears and this allowed her to feel less awkward and exposed when talking to him.

Shari was a young woman when she decided to convert to Judaism. She had been exposed to Judaism on her college campus, and over time came to realize she was truly a seeker. She had never been totally at home in Catholicism even though she was a devoted follower. Shari loved the emphasis on the direct connection each person could have with God, and came to see the role of the priest as unnecessary and even more, as an impediment. She had read about how Rabbi Nachman of Breslov used to go out into the forest and speak out loud to God for one hour each day. She began to use her private time in her dorm room to speak out loud to God the way she had done with her Catholic priest.

On the day of Shari's conversion, she felt prepared and excited. She had not expected to feel self conscious at all during the mikveh ritual. She was surprised to find herself uncomfortable during the process of reciting the blessings after each of her immersions. After finishing, Shari related that her discomfort was about having the rabbis on the other side of the door listening as she dunked. Shari understood the idea of the ritual was to stand before God without any pretense and without anything between her and God. However, Shari explained that for her, having people behind the door felt as if they were eavesdropping on her private and personal encounter with God. It reminded her a lot of confession, which was something she had once loved but had given up in place of something else.

Shari remarked after her immersion that next time she would

like a private conversation with God without the listening ears of the rabbis. ✐

> *Trust in God with all your heart and lean not on your*
> *own understanding; in all your ways acknowledge God,*
> *and God will direct your paths.*
>> *Proverbs 3:5-6*

Louise

*L*ouise, a tall brunette with startling blue eyes, came to the mikveh as a convert to Judaism.

"We've been living a Jewish life since my husband and I married and I have always thought of myself as Jewish. I knew I would eventually convert at some point but it didn't seem the right moment until now. My two teenage sons converted when they were infants and now that my younger son is becoming a Bar Mitzvah soon, I want to formally convert. I need to be a part of his ceremony and to declare myself as officially Jewish."

Louise spoke with passion and conviction. "I chose Channukah as the perfect time for me to complete the ritual because this holiday always had special meaning for me. Even before I met my husband, I truly admired the small band of Maccabees who fought against all odds to acquire religious freedom for their people. This is the holiday I most identify with and want it to mark my becoming Jewish."

With these words Louise went into the changing room and prepared for her immersion. ✐

Every person has their moment.
Pirkei Avot 4:3

Mindy

My mikveh day was a day of affirmation. It was a final purifying moment to join the Jewish community as an official and fully-vested member. During each of my ritual immersions, I reflected on what had brought me to this place and where I would see my Jewish identity leading me in the future. I fondly recalled my *Bet Din* and my personal statement about why I wanted to become Jewish. I started to come up with the sorts of phrases that would fit on a bumper sticker. This led to:

"Top 10 Reasons Why I am Converting"

10. I am converting to Judaism because I feel it is the right thing to do.
9. I've been saying I would convert for the past twenty-five or thirty years.
8. I have been living a basically Jewish life for the last twenty-five or thirty years.
7. Even before *that*, most of my friends and housemates were Jewish.
6. Everybody assumes I'm Jewish.
5. I assume I'm Jewish
4. I know a lot of Jewish people. They are all different. I'm different too!
3. The food!
2. Klezmer music!
1. One more Jewish person in the world is a good thing.

But this isn't something that can be expressed in a few words. It is a commitment to having deep roots and spreading branches. The roots are in my family—Lisa, my wife, and I were living Jewishly long before our son David was born, and we agreed that if we had any children, we would raise them in a Jewish household. We have, and this has led to lots of branches—an ever expanding network of friends, contacts, and organizations for all three of us. ✐

She is a tree of life to those who hold fast to her.
Proverbs 3:18

Stacey

*I*n his Superman cape, Evan flew through the synagogue halls a few yards in front of his parents. Gabe, Stacey's husband, accompanying an eight-and-a-half-months pregnant Stacey on his arm, came to celebrate Stacey and Evan's conversion. Stacey heaved a sigh of relief as she eased into the comfortable waiting room chair. She told me she'd been moving toward conversion for many years.

"I want to convert to Judaism with all I've got. I can't do this half way. This decision to become Jewish will unite my family," she said while Evan tugged at her skirt. Gabe perused our mikveh library and Stacey continued her story. She explained to me how she wanted to give this decision the respect and the full heart it deserved.

"I'm ready to put my whole self into this conversion."

Evan suddenly lost his patience with the lack of attention and interrupted our conversation to tell me about his new friend Julie, who mom quietly explained was imaginary.

"I told Julie that my mom was going to the mikveh because she was low on Jewish and had to get filled." Evan's delightful personality continued to bubble as he told me what the new baby's name would be. "If it's a boy, it will be called Corduroy. If it's a girl, it will be called Queen Esther."

As she immersed, Stacey was beautiful as only a woman holding new life can be. After her immersions she lingered in the water a few extra moments, savoring the weightless feeling. Then it was time for Evan's immersion, and mom put on her bathing suit and assisted him into the mikveh. With the help of his imaginary friend Julie, Evan was ready for the ceremony.

After guiding Evan for his three immersions, and reciting the prayers for her son, Stacey had performed her first religious obligation and bagun her new life as a Jew by helping to bring her son into the fold. ☙

Where you go, I will go; and where you live, I will live;
your people shall be my people, and your God my God.
Ruth 1:16

Dolores

Cindy and Marc arrived with baby Macayla wrapped in the blanket knitted by Cindy's mother, Dolores. Macayla, at only three months, was one of the youngest conversion immersions I had ever overseen. Macayla, tucked into her car seat with the blanket over her, slept on as we all watched and sighed at her sweet face making the little, involuntary movements infants make as they doze.

Dolores, who had arrived in her own car, was thrilled to see Cindy and Marc had brought the blanket she had knit. Dolores and I chatted as Cindy took the sleepy Macayla out of her car seat, preparing her for the immersion.

Dolores exclaimed to me, "Can you believe today is the three-month birthday of my precious little granddaughter? She has already brought so much love and joy into our entire family and especially to me, as her grandmother."

Cindy, Marc, and the rest of their friends and family gathered in the immersion room, along with several rabbis close to the family. As people filed into the room, Macayla became more alert. It was a joyous and meaningful immersion and Macayla only cried a little, settling down right after being dried off and wrapped back in her grandmother's knitted blanket.

Dolores revealed that she too had chosen Judaism twenty years before. She shared a few details of her experience with me and then finished by saying, "My background as a convert made me feel even more blessed as I watched Macayla become a member of the Jewish people. Today I am surrounded by four rabbis, friends, and family. It is probably the most perfect moment in my entire life!" ✐

We acknowledge with thanks that you are Adonai, our God and the God of our ancestors, forever.

Traditional Morning Service,
Modim Blessing of Gratitude

Li Mei

*L*isa and Todd had waited a long time to receive the news they would be traveling to China to unite with their new daughter, Li Mei. Over the months, they had been heartbroken to receive a solitary photo here and there accompanied by news of yet another delay in the adoption process. Together, Lisa and Todd attended to the phone calls and communications with the adoption agency. Since they didn't know when they would be allowed to go to China to bring home their daughter, nor did they know how long the process would take once they arrived, they could not prepare a conversion ceremony with their rabbi in advance.

Some people might be surprised to discover it is not an easy task to schedule a mikveh for conversion. Scheduling requires the coordination of parents, rabbis, friends, relatives, and our own mikveh schedule. When people call for appointments, we always try to accommodate them. However, we are certain to reassure them that a mikveh conversion rarely falls under the category of mikveh emergency. This situation, however, was a true mikveh emergency!

It was a Tuesday when Lisa and Todd came back from China with their precious five-month-old daughter. Early on Wednesday morning, I answered a call from them.

Lisa, who was also a convert, said to me, "We need to come to the mikveh. We want to come to the mikveh now, before Shabbat. We want our little girl to be Jewish as we light Shabbat candles this week!"

Even though I didn't know anything about Lisa and Todd, I could tell by their sense of urgency they had been through tough trials. They needed this moment to transform their experience into one of calm. Fortunately, we were able to arrange for Li Mei to join the Jewish people before Shabbat. ✐

Do not fear, for I am with you; do not anxiously look about you, for I am your God.
Isaiah 41:10

Shelly

Shelly brought three friends to accompany her to the mikveh on her conversion day.

"Where's the line of people?"

"Is the water really cold?"

"It's rain water, right?" they asked her.

"Don't worry," I explained to each of them, "Shelly's immersion will definitely be the only one happening while you are here today, although I do have other immersions after you leave."

The women walked through the mikveh observing the beautiful tiles on the floor and on the walls, and how the rainwater was collected and heated like a pool.

"Wow," Kathy said, "it's so different from what I thought it would be!"

As the tour of the mikveh continued, Annette watched with curiosity, and Shelly nervously clutched her purse to her chest, looking hesitant about going through with the immersion. Despite the tour, Shelly was still feeling apprehensive.

After her immersion, Shelly was much more relaxed.

I received a letter from her, saying,

> *Thank you so much for providing me with an incredible mikveh experience. I won't pretend I wasn't nervous more than I have ever been, but in the end it was truly beautiful. My friends who accompanied me were pleasantly surprised by how beautiful, intimate, and special the ritual was. I think they expected a line of people waiting to get dunked in a very rigid and ceremonially perfunctory sort of way. Thank you for this wonderful experience.* ✑

It is a fountain in the garden, a well of living waters.

Song of Songs 4:15

Reina

R eina clutched her towel around her nervously. Despite her obvious enthusiasm about the experience of mikveh, she was still a self-conscious twelve year old. Her mother, Eileen, had converted to Judaism many years before but had never immersed in the mikveh. She joined her daughter on this special day in preparation for Reina's Bat Mitzvah.

Reina's neon-colored polish was conspicuously absent, but her sunny personality shined through brightly on its own.

Reina admitted to me, "I think inside the mikveh, I will feel safe and a little closer to God. It's going to be a new experience for me and I think it's going to be very spiritual. When I go in the water, I will feel renewed."

Reina's experience did not disappoint her. "The room was warm and I felt warmed and surrounded by God. The warmth inside the mikveh reminded me of a *tallit*, wrapping me with warmth and safety."

Eileen's experience was equally powerful. Visiting the mikveh prepared her to feel Jewishly complete as she would present her daughter with her real *tallit*, a Jewish prayer shawl, on the special Shabbat morning of her public Torah reading.

"Coming to the mikveh was a big thing for me," she reiterated, "it was transformative. I knew I needed to cross all my t's and dot all my i's when it came to being Jewish."

Eileen had been aware she needed to take the next step in her Jewish journey for quite a while. "This ritual has brought us closer as we are looking forward to celebrating a joyous time together at Reina's Bat Mitzvah." ✑

I am going out one door and shall go through another.
　　　Ba'al Shem Tov

Celebration

Chapter 5

Sima

*A*lthough Sima remembers accompanying her mother on her monthly mikveh visits in the former Soviet Union, this would be her first personal experience, as she marked her seventy-fifth birthday. She may have had a Russian accent, but her command of the English language and her vocabulary were inspiring. Sima had lived an intellectual, yet uneventful life in Russia. She married and was a busy mother raising two young children, but she possessed an adventurous spirit. She influenced her husband enough so when the opportunity presented itself, the family would move to America. She wanted to raise her children in a country where they could experience religious and personal freedom as well as pursue their own dreams.

And so they made the move to the United States. The adjustment was difficult for all of them, yet they were survivors and fighters, and they persevered. The family was blessed with a third child, born in Philadelphia. Tragically, only a short time after, Sima's husband passed away and she found herself in the difficult position of being a single parent.

During this dark time, life was challenging for the whole family. They had no relatives in America and only a few friends. But Sima was not one to give up. She worked hard, made sacrifices, and triumphed. She had come here to fulfill a dream, and indeed she did. Her children married and eventually she became a mother-in-law, a grandmother, and a great-grandmother.

She brought to mind her achievements and now she needed to acknowledge herself with prayer and gratitude. Coming up with a celebratory plan was not difficult. The mikveh immersion practice her mother adhered to so many years ago drew her back to its healing waters. There was no doubt, no conflict, and no questioning. She stepped into the water, confident this was the only way for her to communicate her appreciation for the life she had been granted.

When she emerged, I asked her, "What were you able to take

from this experience?"

"Tsk, tsk," she responded wagging her finger. "It's not what I took, it's what I was able to leave, and that was also one of the many blessings in my life." ᴄ⌒ꝋ

> *How fitting it is to praise God's name with gratitude.*
> *Psalms 92:1*

Iris

*I*ris is an energetic woman, always eager to try new things, and a "true New Yorker." As the daughter of immigrants, she'd had a rough start growing up. To the degree that she tried, she always felt she didn't fit into American culture. She was embarrassed by her parents' Yiddish accents and Old World behavior, silently wishing her parents would not speak to her teachers or her friends, and feared they would expose her as the immigrant she truly was.

Her family lived in poverty with the generation gap further widened because her Polish-born parents were not like others. While many new immigrants wanted to Americanize, such as going to night school to learn English, Iris's parents had no desire to change their way of life. They longed for the Old World and felt mixed about their decision to come to the United States. This was evident even in the way Iris looked; she had braids when all her peers wore short bobs and she wore cotton stockings instead of bobby socks. And unlike the other children who rode the bus, her mother stood in front of the school at the end of the day waiting to walk home with her. She was just different.

After Iris's parents passed away, she became drawn to Yiddish culture in a way she had never been before. Although she associated her past with negative memories, she eventually came to terms with her Polish and Jewish heritages. She learned briefly about the tradition of mikveh in a Yiddish book club she attended, and was surprised to discover there was a mikveh nearby.

Iris decided to celebrate her seventieth birthday at the mikveh, and later shared with me, "I am eager to begin again. In spite of the fact I did not have a happy childhood, my experiences shaped me and made me who I am. If you don't feel contented growing up in this world, you can always begin again. The mikveh opened new doors for me. I feel more connected to my past and true self. I feel more connected to God and to my parents." ⌒

A person is not old until their regrets take the place of their dreams.

Yiddish Proverb

Sylvia

*I*t's a warm June afternoon and the phone has been ringing all day with calls about pre-wedding mikveh use. The woman on the phone with me, Sylvia, seems at first to be a typical first-timer to the mikveh. She is curious about using the mikveh before her fortieth wedding anniversary celebration. But as I listen more closely, I realize what I already know to be true; there is no such thing as a *typical* mikveh phone call. More and more meaningful lifecycle events swirl into the conversation, with the potential for holy moments heavy in the air.

"My son's wedding is also coming up, so I would like to use the mikveh to celebrate that as well," she explains.

As I take in the beauty of the fact that her son will be married in the same season in which she was married forty years earlier, she takes a deep breath and blurts, "My nephew died a month ago, and I am expecting a new grandchild in two weeks."

The intersection of life and death, and joy and mourning, is palpable and overwhelming. I provide space for her to talk about what the mikveh will mean to her.

She says, "I don't consider myself a spiritual woman, but I need to mark this special time in my life." I surmise she really *is* a spiritual woman and has not yet realized it. However, she wants this immersion to remain private and doesn't plan to tell anyone about her experience.

Two weeks later, I accompany Sylvia into the mikveh. As she immerses, she recites prayers in her heart—prayers I can only imagine to encompass the joy of new beginnings and the pain of loss—prayers about transition. After completing three immersions, I hold up her robe, signaling she can leave the water.

Sylvia hesitates a moment and I suggest to her, "Why don't you stay in the water a little longer?" She nods. I put down her robe and leave the room.

I find Sylvia's story courageous, inspiring, meaningful, and spiritual. While Sylvia may not have entered the mikveh as a "spiritual woman," she certainly left as one. ∽

> *The world is new to us every morning and each person should believe they are reborn each day.*
> *Ba'al Shem Tov*

Elaine

Sometimes mikveh immersions mark a rite of passage, as was the case with Elaine. She visited the mikveh to mark a special birthday: seventy-five. She radiated gratitude, not just for having reached this milestone, but for the way in which she was able to reach it. Elaine had been born in the United States, and embraced the freedom, good health, happy family, and the charmed life she had been granted.

Elaine's friends encouraged her to celebrate this special birthday with a trip to a luxury spa, or a weekend in New York to attend a Broadway show and dine on delectable cuisine. Although she appreciated all the gifts granted to her, Elaine knew she needed a uniquely Jewish spiritual experience. A trip to the spa or to New York City did not satisfy her yearning. She had heard of the mikveh and even had friends who had used the mikveh to mark moments in their own lives. The renewing water of the mikveh was the best choice in her mind.

Elaine came to the mikveh, traveling with a purpose and a clear goal. It was evident she knew exactly what she wanted from her mikveh experience.

Elaine's immersion had been a deeply meaningful venture for her and she shared a brief part of it with me via a thank-you note…

> I was full of seemingly contradictory emotions, both while I was in the mikveh, and for some time afterward: singularity and peoplehood, anticipation and reflection, comfort and being on the edge of comfort, novelty and the arc of history, and finally, simple exhilaration!
>
> The readings you chose for me were a beautiful way of helping me come to the new experience with dignity, purpose, and kavanah. I feel entirely cleansed, renewed, and ready to begin a new chapter in my life. ✐
>
> Thankfulness has an inner connection with humility. It recognizes that what we are and what we have is due to others and above all, God.
> Rabbi Jonathan Sacks

Celebration

Rosalie

*I*t was a busy week. I spent time baking the traditional round challah for Rosh Hashana, made soups and cakes for our family to eat, searched the market for pomegranates, and critiqued my husband's sermons, helping him prepare for the holiday. The trouble was, it was an incredibly busy time at the mikveh as well. I worried I wouldn't be able to focus on Rosalie's immersion, and it was important that I be present for her – especially since it was her first time at the mikveh.

Rosalie, in her fifties, declared to me over the phone, "I want to go to the mikveh before Rosh Hashana to help prepare me to celebrate the New Year." Upon her arrival, she appeared unsettled.

"The High Holiday preparation is painful for me," she explained, "It's much more complicated than welcoming the sweetness of new beginnings."

After showering and preparing her mind and body in the preparation room, she approached the mikveh. Rosalie promptly sat down on the steps and began reading some of the materials I provide for each mikveh user. She seemed completely absorbed in a small book by Rebbe Nachman of Breslov. As is my custom as an attendant, I always leave the room in order to give each person the opportunity to spend time alone.

Returning to the mikveh room, we spoke again.

"I doubt my worthiness," she confessed, her eyes downcast. "Am I worthy enough to go into the mikveh? Is my coming here prompted by sincere emotions? Am I being myself by coming here? I always associated mikveh attendance with religiously devoted people."

I reassured her she was definitely worthy of using the mikveh. I made clear to her, "We use the mikveh during times of transformation and transition. We are always growing, learning, and changing as Jews. Mikveh is just one way we can feel supported during those times of change."

Rosalie entered the mikveh waters with tears rolling down her face. ◌

God is near to all who call upon God with sincerity.
Psalms 145:18.

157

Beth

*B*eth, a young woman in her thirties, spoke earnestly to me. "You know Lori, I am an English teacher here in Wynnewood, Pennsylvania. I love my job. And I also love Israel. So here is my dilemma: out of the blue, Eric, my husband, was offered a job he can't refuse – an assistant professorship at Bar Ilan University. Sounds great, right? Except it would entail the whole family moving to Israel.

"I'm uncertain I'll find work and the thought of staying home every day is not very attractive. Furthermore, I will have to find a whole new network of friends for myself and schools for the children, and deal with carpooling in a country known for its reckless and impatient drivers, while struggling to read Hebrew street signs with my poor command of the language. I also feel ambivalent about leaving my parents and sisters. Living in Israel has been something I have been dreaming about for years, but faced with the reality, the prospects are overwhelming."

When I asked her about her motivation to visit the mikveh, she revealed she hoped it would support her with the difficult transition. She needed the mikveh experience to move her from fearful skepticism to hopeful anticipation. Understanding her wishes, I let her know many mikveh experiences had brought acknowledgement and reconciliation to many of its users and I anticipated it would do the same for her.

When she emerged, I shared my desire that she received all she needed from the mikveh.

"The mikveh experience was so much more powerful and emotional than I thought it would be," she remarked. "I'm feeling less anxious about the move now that I've immersed inside the mikveh. The mikveh provided me with a framework for my move to Israel and now I feel more enthusiastic and hopeful. Yes, I got exactly what I needed!" ∽

> *Every person should carefully observe which way their heart draws them, and then choose that way with all their strength.*
> *Chassidic Proverb*

Michal

I ought to share the special mikveh experience I had with my mother. As a child and teenager, my mother and I enjoyed a warm, close relationship. I cannot recall a time when we ever fought or stopped talking with each other. I could always share my problems and feelings with her. My mother was always loving, available, helpful, and a source of strength. I thought this relationship would never change.

Our closeness began eroding when I married and moved to the East Coast while she remained in Oregon. She had an intense fear of flying—a fear so great it even put an emotional distance between us. She panicked at the thought of entering an airplane. It took years before she would even come to see us and I had been saddened these visits were so few and far between. Our close-knit relationship slowly unraveled. Although she continued showing great interest in my life, we both struggled with the distance, the time difference, and her fear of flying.

I understood that if I wanted to see my parents and have them see our children, I had to fly out to Oregon; a hardship further intensified by having to travel with three young children. As a result of several years of having to fly out to see my parents, I began to feel alone, and somewhat estranged. I even had feelings of guilt for having moved so far away. After many years of missing the closeness of the other, my mother made a decision to visit my family more often, despite the anxiety it caused. She realized she had missed out on being more of an integral part of our family's and my life.

When I first brought my mother to the mikveh where I was volunteering, she was impressed and awed. She wanted to know more about it and the various uses for it. During one of her visits to see our family, I was surprised when she expressed an interest in sharing the mikveh experience with me. I asked if she was making the request for herself or for me. My mother assured me it was strictly for her. Before entering the pool, we sat together on the bench inside the mikveh room, sharing blessings for each other as we reminisced. Separately, we entered the mikveh waters and immersed on our own, reciting the blessing for arriving at this sacred moment in our lives.

The mikveh gave me a new opportunity to connect with my mother. We prayed for a renewed commitment to each other and to our own lives. We emerged from the mikveh waters with a dedicated desire to strengthen our relationship and embrace one another, despite the distance between us. ✍

All blessings shall come upon you and take effect.

Deuteronomy 28:2

Leyla & Ilana

L eyla and Ilana, partners in a loving and committed marriage, were so excited about coming to the mikveh. They made an appointment to visit the mikveh while in the ninth month of pregnancy. They wanted to pray for an easy delivery and most of all, for a healthy baby.

For over three years, they had appeared before all types of counselors, applying and receiving grants to help them pay for the fertilization process. In spite of multiple attempts at using intrauterine insemination, Leyla was unable to carry a baby to full term. Determined to be parents, Ilana and Leyla never gave up hope on having a baby. The couple agreed it was paramount that Leyla be the one to carry the baby. And so, a decision was made: a fusion of science and a miraculous intervention.

Ilana's egg and a donor's sperm were introduced into Leyla's uterus and eventually they conceived a miracle! Leyla had become pregnant using Ilana's egg–incredibly the baby would be the biological union of both Leyla and Ilana! For so many years they had struggled and now, after finally becoming pregnant, they were ready to celebrate!

Ilana and Leyla arrived at the mikveh together, holding hands and smiling, with Leyla visibly showing the fullness of her nine months. Experiencing the mikveh together was fundamental in their expression of gratitude for their pregnancy.

"Coming to the mikveh is like the 'homestretch,' and the fulfillment of a dream," they verbalized to me after the ritual was over. A week later, Ilana and Leyla became new mothers to a wonderful and healthy baby boy. ∽

L'chaim!
To Life!
       Hebrew phrase of celebration.

Anat

*T*he road to the mikveh is often one with twists and turns. For Anat, her arrival at the mikveh was preceded by heartache and disappointment. For a long time, she and her husband had trouble conceiving, and Anat had already miscarried three times in the past two years. On some level, Anat withheld the sense of joy she had hoped to feel, afraid to connect too closely to her baby, in order to avoid the pain of another excruciating experience.

Anat came to the mikveh, her cheeks glowing, and her skin radiant as though brushed with dew. In her ninth month of pregnancy, she arrived at the mikveh happy, excited. She was eager not only to immerse, but to thank God for allowing her to enjoy an uncomplicated pregnancy and for giving her a sense of well-being. She also came to pray for a healthy baby and an easy delivery.

She entered the pool feeling alive with the new life she carried within her. Anat spent time meditating in the mikveh's calming waters.

"For nearly nine months, I have carried and nurtured you within my life-giving waters. I've wondered how that must feel to you? Today, I am lifted and weightless in the living waters of the mikveh. For the first time, I have a sense about how you must feel as you are soon to make an entrance into this world. I cannot wait to cradle you in my arms."

> *God of patience, help me to learn to wait for the good that will soon be within my reach, that is just a moment away.*
> *Rabbi Nachman of Breslov*

Robin

A woman in her mid-fifties, Robin came out of the changing room wearing a colorful sarong fitting her personality perfectly. Without her bright floral dresses, large beaded necklaces, and fuschia colored lipstick, Robin looked innocent and almost childlike in her comfortable purple tie-dye Hawaiian sarong.

"I love to be dressed for the occasion," Robin mused. "This is the perfect outfit to be wearing to the mikveh." Using both hands, she swept her long hair behind her ears and proceeded toward the mikveh steps.

"Am I really expected to take this off?" she asked at the foot of the stairs.

I explained to her, "As a mikveh attendant, when an immerser walks down the steps of the mikveh, we are all trained to provide as much privacy as possible. We do this in part by helping to remove the sarong or robe the person is wearing and using it to block our vision. We do this so that you have as much privacy as possible as you enter the mikveh pool."

Robin frowned but acquiesced to my request. She had come to the mikveh to prepare herself spiritually. She would be reading Torah for the first time in her life on the coming Shabbat.

"I want to read from the Torah with the proper *kavanah*, or intention," she told me. After immersing, she noted, "I feel prepared and I will be coming back to the mikveh to celebrate other wonderful times in my life."

That Shabbat, I smiled as I listened to Robin reading from the Torah. Her chanting rang beautifully in my ears, enhancing my own *kavanah*. ⌒

I love God, because God has heard my voice, my supplications.

Psalms 116:1

Caryn

*U*pon reaching menopause, Caryn became depressed. She was unprepared for the arrival of this new stage of life. In spite of her recognition that she had been done with childbearing years earlier, there had been something special in her awareness that she could still grow life inside herself if she had wanted to.

Now Caryn felt, well, just old. When her mother died nine months later, this only added to her feeling she was deeply submersed in this new transitional stage in her life. Caryn painfully acknowledged she was no longer the "young" generation. She had been replaced by her children in that role. With both of her parents now deceased, she and her husband were the "old" generation.

It had been a year since she had stopped menstruating and three months since her mother died.

"There have been so many losses in my life during the past year. Not unexpected, but certainly unwelcomed. While feeling sorry for myself, I looked around to see all that I still have. I want to replace my losses by recognizing and appreciating the blessings which are so much a part of my life. I want to look forward to graduations, marriages of my children, and grandparenthood. I came to realize menopause is not the loss of life. My mother's spirit will live in me forever.

"My mother was raised in an Orthodox home. She encouraged us to be proud of our Judaism. In my childhood, there was always a sense of connection to Judaism and tradition but not necessarily strict observance."

Upon emerging from the mikveh, Caryn smiled and shared, "My mother would have been thrilled to know I went to the mikveh."

In the months following, Caryn began to explore other rituals her mother may have once known. In this way, she forged a spiritual connection with the generation past and is looking forward to the future. ∽

Because time itself is like a spiral, something special happens to you on your birthday each year: the same energy that God invested in you at birth is present once again.

Rabbi Menachem Mendel Schneerson

Kelly

*K*elly and her four friends had maintained a close relationship since high school.

"Few people manage to keep friendships alive for so long," Kelly reported to her closest childhood friends. "We have been so lucky to have each other through difficult times as well as in celebration."

Kelly, humorous and outgoing, was unquestionably the leader at initiating contacts, gatherings, and celebrations. Even though they had attended different colleges, they had maintained their closeness for decades.

One of Kelly's friends remarked to me, "During a recent conversation, we wondered at how we could deepen our relationships by marking significant moments in our lives together. We sought a ritual that might help us give tangible significance to the moments we share. Kelly, a monthly immerser, told us how meaningful her experiences at the mikveh have been. She came up with this idea of coming to the mikveh and creating a ritual to mark the commitment we ourselves make to each other."

Only hours before Yom Kippur night, Kelly and her friends visited the mikveh.

"This is the perfect time for all of us to express our gratitude for having each other and enjoying all that life has offered us. This is the perfect place to chart our course for our future as friends forever."

They entered the waters one at a time and afterward joined hands, celebrating with songs and laughter. ✑

Blessed are those who bless you.

Numbers 24:9

Marilyn, Bonnie, and Nancy

*M*arilyn, Bonnie, and Nancy had been friends for years, ever since their children attended nursery school together. Marilyn, a teacher, Bonnie, a lawyer, and Nancy, a financial advisor, not only had children at the same, but they also shared October birthdays. For years, the three of them celebrated their birthdays together by going to lunch and ordering extravagant desserts.

At the time of their sixtieth birthdays, Bonnie suggested that since this was a milestone birthday, they change their routine.

"How about going to the mikveh to share in our gratitude for having reached this occasion, having remained friends, having enjoyed each other's joys and sadness, and most of all, for being blessed with good health."

None of them had ever been to the mikveh before and initially Nancy seemed apprehensive. "I don't see why we should go to the mikveh. Why can't we have an elaborate dinner instead?"

"No, I think the mikveh is a great idea. I think a spiritual marking takes our milestone out of the ordinary and gives it special meaning. I like the idea," Marilyn advocated.

Bonnie and Marilyn came to scout out the mikveh before making the appointment.

"Nancy, you are going to love it," Marilyn reported back to Nancy after their tour. "The mikveh is beautiful, clean, and inviting. Although the mikveh has been around for centuries, it is as relevant today as it was over two thousand years ago."

"Okay, " Nancy reluctantly complied. "You've got me sold. But we can still have the big dinner after the mikveh."

They sat on the mikveh steps together, reading to themselves and to each other the literature they had carefully preselected about aging and change. Each woman eventually immersed privately with Lori as her attendant. After the immersions, they all joined inside the soothing room containing the sacred waters of the mikveh and recited the *Shehecheyanu* together.

As they dried their hair, reapplied their makeup, and adorned themselves with jewelry, Nancy declared, "This was a very special day for us."

Bonnie thoughtfully added, "It added depth and meaning and a spiritual dimension to our aging process."

Marilyn, the quietest of the three, nodded with pleasure, breathing a sigh of relief. Since the whole thing had been her idea, she was pleased it all worked out. ✐

Thirty, for strength.
Forty, for understanding.
Fifty, for counsel.
Sixty, for sagacity.
Seventy, for elderliness.
Eighty, for power.
> *Pirkei Avot 5:21*

Tovah

*T*he first community where I served as a rabbi was exceptionally warm and welcoming. I know that this culture was built over years under the leadership of a beloved rabbi and many loving lay leaders. I was twenty-seven years old when I arrived, and though I had been at JTS for nine years, it was my congregants who taught me how to be a rabbi. They were led by kindness. We learned together. We did *tikkun* together. We called out to the Holy One of Blessing together. We grew together.

After almost seven years together, we decided that it was time to sunset the shul. The neighborhood had changed dramatically; the finances were difficult. We still had many devoted members. Some of our people lived in the area, but the majority of our folks had moved out of the neighborhood. Together, we decided to leave our building and join our small sacred community with a larger, suburban, more affluent community. This small shul felt somewhat like a "Garden of Eden" of shuls to me, and to others. And you don't generally move Eden, you leave it.

For almost a year, I had many conversations with my people listening to their communal pain and trying to help them accept this decision. Many of the older people had literally gone door to door selling bricks for their new post-World War II shul. Many younger families had found a loving, joyous, accepting place to be Jewish. Our Eden was one of all sorts: twenty-six kids going to Jewish summer camp, spirited services, social justice projects. A "can-do" and "let's help each other" spirit was imbued in the fabric of the place.

For me, closing was about the finances and the future—but the present was a successful Jewish community. If you measure success on the amount of Torah, worship, and good deeds that emanate from a place, then our congregation was absolutely a success! We found a wonderful place to take us in. But it would not ever be the same.

We moved B'nai Mitzvah dates. We checked Torah scrolls. We decided what would come with us. But in the end, the hardest changes to navigate were the differences in culture. Our leaders accepted that for the most part they would not be big fish in the pond. People began to come to grips with the idea that they would be from "the shul that closed." I fully admit that we could have remained open for more years, but the elders of the shul were convinced that it would be better for the younger families if we moved en masse, to a place with more young families and more resources. So, they made the hard decision to close and to merge.

And in the end, I would be going with our community. It would be new for me also.

There were lots more discussions with sad members. I was trying to hold their pain, but quite frankly, that meant not dealing with mine. How was I going to be okay leaving Eden?

And so, the week before we closed the shul with a weekend of commemoration and a moving ceremony, I quietly went to work on my own *neshama*, my spirit. I went to immerse in The Mikveh at Temple Beth Hillel-Beth El.

I had loved my first experience immersing in a mikveh. It was back in New York, seven years earlier, on the eve of my ordination. All of the women in my class had gone. It was now time to be renewed. It was again time to return to the waters, to the Holy One of Blessing. It was time to again access the spiritually healing waters.

I had taken so many women to mikveh, as brides, for conversion, and for healing ceremonies. Now, I needed someone who could guide me as I had guided others. Lori Cooper, the mikveh founder and director, would be my guide. Lori had shepherded so many people through mikveh experiences. Lori knew what living in a rabbinic family was. Lori knew that the mikveh could be a place to leave sadness and fear—or at least accept it, so I knew she would be the one to help me.

I was sad and scared; I cried for the loss of my community.

Even in the traditional world, mikveh has connotations for the individual of acknowledging loss and then being renewed. I was here at the mikveh to confront both my personal and communal loss, and to hopefully find a sense of renewal. I cried for what my beautiful people were losing.

I prepared myself slowly, listening to my Jewish *a capella* group. There are no traditional blessings to immerse in a mikveh as a way of spiritually finding healing, but Lori brought poems, psalms, and readings. She allowed me to metaphorically leave my tears in the mikveh. Each step into the water was about embracing the sadness and the fear. Immersing myself fully in the water itself felt like a catharsis. I could leave the tears here. I could be renewed by this renewing water. I sang psalms and they reverberated in the personal, cathedral-like, echo chamber of the mikveh. And each of the seven steps up and out of the mikveh seemed to build new resolve in me. Resolve that in the end, you can move parts of Eden.

Eden, with its primordial waters, represents our capacity to see beauty and the potential of newness. It is even our ability to hold and then let go of fear and pain. The mikveh helped me begin to see how letting go would allow me to move forward. ✍

Help me to understand that my vulnerabilities in fact open me to growth; my limits draw me to new frontiers; my very failures teach me to succeed.

Rabbi Nachman of Breslov

Alexandra

*R*obin had studied Judaism for a year and toured the mikveh before her final conversion. Even so, she never expected she would be filled with such a sense of belonging after her mikveh experience. As a recent convert, Robin had been talking about the mikveh and telling her friend Alexandra what a powerful experience it was—certainly the highlight of her conversion process. Robin was so moved by the experience, she informed Alexandra she planned to return before Rosh HaShanah.

Alexandra shrugged her shoulders and exclaimed, "What's Rosh Hashanah?! For me, it's sitting in a crowded synagogue surrounded by people I don't know and listening to prayers I can't relate to. I don't feel God's presence on Rosh Hashanah or any other holiday."

"Trust me," Robin asserted, "During my mikveh experience, I was very well aware of God's presence. Alexandra, you have nothing to lose and you just might find something you are looking for."

Alexandra was doubtful but willing to try. She stepped into the water with skepticism and emerged pleasantly surprised.

"The water was warm, soothing, and allowed me to release all my doubts. I found inspiration for the new year. And although I did not find God's presence in the room, I did feel comforted."

I reminded Alexandra the waters are not magic but they are powerful and suggested she might benefit by coming again.

"Yes, I think I will," she concurred. ✑

God searches all hearts on the day of the Jewish New Year.
L'eyl Orech Din, Traditional Rosh HaShanah prayer.

Celia

Celia had a difficult time getting to the mikveh. She didn't have a car, and although she was only sixty-four years old, she wasn't in the best of health and didn't live near public transportation. Her daughter, Karen, who normally took her to medical appointments and helped with her shopping, was dismissive of her mother's "new-born" Judaism. Celia approached me about her predicament. While it is not normally my practice to get involved in the personal lives of my clients, I asked if I might be permitted to contact someone who could help her.

Celia had taken a renewed interest in Judaism and was studying with a rabbi who had primarily referred her to the mikveh to mark her return to Judaism. I called the rabbi to see if he could help Celia. Fortunately, the rabbi sought out Esther, a volunteer in the community, to give Celia rides when needed.

Esther shared some of her past with Celia, confiding that she had converted to Judaism five years earlier, and congratulated Celia for taking the opportunity to have her own mikveh immersion experience.

"I'm curious about your visit," Esther revealed, "What made you come to the mikveh even though you are already Jewish?"

"I wanted a concrete experience to mark my return to Judaism," Celia admitted.

After Celia's immersion, she reflected on her experience. "I felt as if I were in a protected environment. Mikveh is a reaffirmation for me. Judaism has added a remarkable dimension to my life. I wish I had been able to impart this beautiful religion to my children. On some level, I feel my indifference to Judaism deprived them of a spiritual and religious connection to their rich past."

"I feel the same way about my son," Esther interjected, "But hopefully our children will come to their roots the same way we did."

The two of them smiled and said in unison, "I guess it's never too late."

It was a shared, intimate moment as the two harmoniously nodded and departed together. The beginning of their friendship rooted with sacred moments and talks about motherhood. ∽

I am still confident of this: I will see the goodness of God in the land of the living.
          Psalms 27:13

Yonit

*W*e leave *Mitzrayim*,
the narrow place,
and come to the shores of the sea.

Frightened,
we cannot imagine going forward.
The pull to return is intense—like a tidal current.
Afraid of drowning.
Afraid of arriving.
Afraid of the unknown.

Miriam says to us,
"Have no fear,
stand still and see the possibilities of transformation in the dividing waters,
the enveloping wind,
and in the starlit sky above us."
Then Miriam turns and utters a wordless plea for help
 and suddenly we are urged to journey forward.

And we journey across the sea,
into the unknown wilderness,
together,
finding comfort in the touching between our bodies,
finding courage in hearing our voices,
the timbrels and the bells,
in the mystery of our breath
finding *bitachon* – confidence in keeping pace with each others' spirits.

We know each other as women.
We see each other clearly,
we love each other through our struggles and our pain,

we love each other through our becoming.

We know you, Yonit, as women know a woman.
We see you clearly,
we love you in your struggles and your pain,
we love you in all of life's seasons.

This is the way in which we are visible to each other,
this is the way you make *Shechinah* visible to us.

Traveling together,
it would be hard to see *Shechinah* without you, Yonit.
We see *Shechinah* in the twinkle of your eye,
we hear *Shechinah* in the way in which you tell your stories,
we learn from *Shechinah* through your wise teachings,
we feel *Shechinah* in your presence, in your power, and in your fragility.

We witness your becoming,
and your becoming is our becoming.

Together we leave *Mitzrayim*,
together we reach the promised land. ✑

> *From every human being there rises a light.*
> *Ba'al Shem Tov*

Quotation
Listings

The following is a list of quotations and excerpts found within this book. Wherever possible, citations are given in English.

BIBLICAL SOURCES

"May God bless you and guard you. May God make his face shine upon you and be gracious to you. May God watch over you and bless you with peace."
Numbers 6:24, page 32

"Isaac dug anew the wells that had been dug by his father Abraham."
Genesis 26:16, page 34

"Make me a Sanctuary so that I might dwell in it."
Exodus 25:8, page 35

"May the voices of joy and gladness, of groom and bride yet be heard in the streets of Jerusalem."
Jeremiah 33:10-11, page 36

"Even raging waters cannot extinguish the fires of love."
Song of Songs 2:18, page 37

"As face answers to face in water, so does one person's heart to another."
Proverbs 27:19, page 39

"This is the day the Holy One has made, let us rejoice and be glad in it."
Psalms 118:24, page 40

"I remember what it was like to be in love when I was young."
Jeremiah 2:2, page 42

"Delight yourself in God and God will give you the desires of your heart."
Psalms 37:4, page 45

"It is not good for a person to be alone."
Genesis 2:18, page 49

"A time for lovers, come to my garden."
Song of Songs 7:13, page 66

"May this be an acceptable time for my prayer."
Psalms 69:14, page 69

"Be fertile and increase and fill the earth."
Genesis 1:28, page 71

"God remembered Sarah and God did as God had spoken."
Genesis 21:1, page 74

"For I will pour water on the thirsty land, and streams on the dry ground; I will pour my Spirit on your offspring, and my blessing on your descendants."
Isaiah 44:3, page 82

"'For I know the plans I have for you,' says God. 'They are plans for good and not for disaster, to give you a future and a hope.'"
Jeremiah 29:11, page 86

"The left hand is under my head and the right arm embraces me."
Song of Songs 2:6, page 87

"God will take us back in love, God will cover up our iniquities and dunk your sins into the depths of the sea."
Micah 7:19, page 89

"When I am afraid, I put my trust in you. In God, whose word I praise —in God, I trust and am not afraid."
Psalms 56:4-5, page 91

"Cast your burden upon God, and God will sustain you."
Psalms 55:23, page 92

"A Song of Ascents. I lift up my eyes to the hills. From where does my help come? My help comes from God, who made heaven and earth."
Psalms 121:1, page 93

"Please God, please God, heal her."
Numbers 12:13, page 94

"Hear, O God, and be merciful to me; O God, be my help. You turned my wailing into dancing; you removed my sackcloth and clothed me with joy, that my heart may sing to you and not be silent. O God my God, I will give You thanks forever."
Psalms 30:11-13, page 95

"Strengthen yourselves, and God will give your heart courage, all of you who hope in God."
Psalms 31:25, page 97

"God is my light and my salvation; Whom shall I fear? God is the strength of my life; Of whom shall I be afraid?"
Psalms 27:1, page 100

*"Shema Yisrael,
Adonai Eloheinu,
Adonai Echad!
Listen, people of Israel, our God is One God!"*
Deuteronomy 6:4, page 101

"Help us to return to You and renew our days as of old."
    Lamentations 5:21, page 102

"God gives strength to the weary and increases the power of the weak. Even youths grow tired and weary, and young men stumble and fall; but those who hope in God will renew their strength. They will soar on wings like eagles; they will run and not grow weary, they will walk and not be faint."
    Isaiah 40:20-31, page 105

"O my God, I cried out to You, and You have healed me."
    Psalms 30:3, page 106

"Show me your ways, God, teach me your paths."
    Psalms 25:4, page 117

"Then Hannah prayed and said, 'My heart exults in God.'"
    1 Samuel 2:1, page 119

"And the sea split before them and they passed through on dry land."
    Nehemiah 9:11, page 123

"To everything there is a season, and a time for every purpose under Heaven: a time to keep silence and a time to speak."
    Eclesiastes 3:1 and 7, page 126

"Shout for joy to God, all the earth."
    Psalms 100:1, page 127

"We prayed for this child and God has granted us what we asked."
    1 Samuel 1:127, page 132

"Happy is she who dwells in Thy house...."
    Psalms 145:1, page 138

"Trust in God with all your heart and lean not on your own understanding; in all your ways acknowledge God, and God will direct your paths."
    Proverbs 3:5-6, page 140

"She is a tree of life to those who hold fast to her."
    Proverbs 3:18, page 142

"Where you go, I will go; and where you live, I will live; your people shall be my people, and your God, my God."
    Ruth 1:16, page 143

"Do not fear, for I am with you; do not anxiously look about you, for I am your God."
    Isaiah 41:10, page 145

"It is a fountain in the garden, a well of living waters."
Song of Songs 4:15, page 146

"How fitting it is to praise God's name with gratitude."
Psalms 92:1, page 152

"God is near to all who call upon God with sincerity."
Psalms 145:18, page 157

"All blessings shall come upon you and take effect."
Deuteronomy 28:2, page 160

"I love God, because God has heard my voice, my supplications."
Psalms 116:1, page 163

"Blessed are those who bless you...."
Numbers 24:9, page 165

"I am still confident of this: I will see the goodness of God in the land of the living."
Psalms 27:13, page 173

RABBINIC SOURCES

"Great is peace since all blessings are in it."
Leviticus Rabah, 9:9, page 48

"A husband and wife are one soul, separated only through their descent to this world. When they are married, they are reunited again."
Zohar 191a, page 59

"To the One whose goodness renews Creation daily."
Traditional Morning Service, Yotzer Or Blessing, page 63

"Each according to their strength."
Midrash Mekhilta de Rabbi Yishmael, BaChodesh 9
on Psalms 29:4, page 67

"May my heart and body always sing praises to the living God."
Traditional Shabbat Song, page 68

"May we rejoice forever in the words of Your Torah and Your commandments."
Traditional Evening Service, Ahavah Rabah Blessing, page 70

"Let the loving couple be very happy just as You made Your creation happy in the Garden of Eden so long ago."
5th Wedding Blessing of the Sheva Berachot, page 72

"The gates of tears are never locked."
Talmud Berachot 32b, page 81

"Blessed is the Source of all in the Universe, who has given us life, sustained us, and enabled us to reach this moment."
Shehecheyanu Blessing, page 84

"Hope for a miracle, but don't depend on it."
Talmud Megillah 7b, page 116

"In the name of Adonai, the God of Israel:
May the angel Michael be at my right,
and the angel Gabriel be at my left;
and in front of me the angel Uriel,
and behind me the angel Raphael . . .
and above my head the Sh'khinat El, the Divine Presence."
From the Bedtime "Shema" Prayer, page 121

"When one comes to be converted, receive them with an open hand, so that they can come under the wings of the Divine Presence."
Leviticus Rabah 2:9, page 131

"As my family planted for me, so do I plant for my children."
Talmud Tractate Ta'anit 23a, page 135

"Every person has their moment."
Pirkei Avot 4:3, page 141

"We acknowledge with thanks that you are Adonai, our God and the God of our ancestors, forever."
Traditional Morning Service, Modim Blessing of Gratitude, page 144

"Thirty, for strength. Forty, for understanding. Fifty, for counsel. Sixty, for sagacity. Seventy, for elderliness. Eighty, for power."
Pirkei Avot 5:21, page 167

"God searches all hearts on the day of the Jewish New Year."
L'eil Orech Din, Traditional Rosh Hashanah Prayer, page 171

CHASSIDIC SOURCES

"All beginnings require that you unlock new doors."
Rabbi Nachman of Breslov, page 51

"Let every lonely and incomplete soul know the wholeness of being that comes when one finds one's love."
Rabbi Nachman of Breslov, page 64

"If you are not a better person today than you were yesterday, what need have you for tomorrow."
Rabbi Nachman of Breslov, page 77

"You are wherever your thoughts are. Make sure your thoughts are where you want to be."
Rabbi Nachman of Breslov, page 103

"O loving God, help me discover and uncover all that is good, all that is positive in the world."
Rabbi Nachman of Breslov, page 109

"The world is a narrow bridge, the main thing is not to be afraid."
Rabbi Nachman of Breslov, page 114

"Prayers truly from the heart open all doors in heaven."
Rabbi Nachman of Breslov, page 134

"Dear God, teach me to begin anew, to renew myself with all of creation."
Rabbi Nachman of Breslov, page 136

"I am going out one door and shall go through another."
Ba'al Shem Tov, page 147

"The world is new to us every morning and each person should believe they are reborn each day."
Ba'al Shem Tov, page 155

"Every person should carefully observe which way their heart draws them, and then choose that way with all their strength."
Chassidic Proverb, page 158

"God of patience, help me to learn to wait for the good that will soon be within my reach, that is just a moment away."
Rabbi Nachman of Breslov, page 162

"Help me to understand that my vulnerabilities in fact open me to growth; my limits draw me to new frontiers; my very failures teach me to succeed."
Rabbi Nachman of Breslov, page 170

"From every human being there rises a light."
Ba'al Shem Tov, page 175

CLASSICAL GREEK SOURCES

"To live life with another is better than no other."
Socrates, page 33

"A human being becomes whole not in virtue of a relation to themself only but rather in virtue of an authentic relation to another human being."
Aristotle, page 50

CONTEMPORARY SOURCES

"May we and all Israel have a favorable omen and good fortune."
Traditional Jewish Folk Song, page 43

"When someone you love becomes a memory, the memory becomes a treasure."
Anonymous, page 44

"When two people relate to each other authentically and humanly, God is the electricity surging between them."
Martin Buber, page 47

"The most beautiful emotion we can experience is the mysterious."
Albert Einstein, page 53

"All journeys have a secret destination of which the traveler is unaware."
Martin Buber, page 58

"When a person immerses their entire being in the water of the Mikveh, 'they leave the ground of humanity and return, for a moment, to the world of elements, in order to begin a new life of purity.' Symbolically they are reborn."
Rabbi Samson Raphael Hirsch,
Commentary on Parashat Shmini, Leviticus 91:11-47, page 60

"God, stay with me through sleepless nights, send me stamina to sustain me, never leave me."
Rabbi Naomi Levy, page 62

"Sometimes the most important things in life don't make sense."
Rabbi Harold Kushner, page 75

"I try to maintain hope, or at least the memory of hope, when I am consumed with fear and despair."
Paul Cowan, *page 85*

"Heal my heart, God. Fill me with strength to gather up all the broken pieces and begin again."
Rabbi Naomi Levy, *page 99*

"Signs of your nearness offer me support and comfort when faced with fear your love flows over me and sustains me."
Psalms 23, *Interpretation by Sheryl Lewart, page 107*

"We come from different places, we may take different paths but we are striving to know the same God."
Anonymous, *page 125*

"The only person you are destined to become is the person you decide to be."
Ralph Waldo Emerson, *page 129*

"All of us have an angel of God calling out to us to show us the way: to blessings, to clarify, and to prophetic vision."
Rabbi Naomi Levy, *page 133*

"A person is not old until their regrets take the place of their dreams."
Yiddish Proverb, *page 153*

"Thankfulness has an inner connection with humility. It recognizes that what we are and what we have is due to others and above all, to God."
Rabbi Jonathan Sacks, *page 156*

"L'chaim!
To Life!"
Hebrew Phrase of Celebration, *page 161*

"Because time itself is like a spiral, something special happens to you on your birthday each year: the same energy that God invested in you at birth is present once again.
Rabbi Menachem Mendel Schneerson, *page 164*

CPSIA information can be obtained
at www.ICGtesting.com
Printed in the USA
BVHW071253070119
537203BV00013B/1511/P

9 780998 049502